T0208436

LIFE'S LITTLE TIDBITS

PAUL and **KATHY HATALSKY**

WESTBOW
PRESS®
A DIVISION OF THOMAS NELSON
& ZONDERVAN

This book is a work of non-fiction. Unless otherwise noted, the author and the publisher make no explicit guarantees as to the accuracy of the information contained in this book and in some cases, names of people and places have been altered to protect their privacy.

WestBow Press books may be ordered through booksellers or by contacting:

WestBow Press
A Division of Thomas Nelson & Zondervan
1663 Liberty Drive
Bloomington, IN 47403
www.westbowpress.com
844-714-3454

Because of the dynamic nature of the Internet, any web addresses or links contained in this book may have changed since publication and may no longer be valid. The views expressed in this work are solely those of the author and do not necessarily reflect the views of the publisher, and the publisher hereby disclaims any responsibility for them.

Any people depicted in stock imagery provided by Getty Images are models, and such images are being used for illustrative purposes only.
Certain stock imagery © Getty Images.

Unless otherwise indicated, all Scripture quotations are taken from the (NASB®) New American Standard Bible®, Copyright © 1960, 1971, 1977, 1995, 2020 by The Lockman Foundation. Used by permission. All rights reserved. www.lockman.org

Scripture marked (KJV) taken from the King James Version of the Bible.

Scripture quotations marked (NLT) are taken from the Holy Bible, New Living Translation, copyright ©1996, 2004, 2015 by Tyndale House Foundation. Used by permission of Tyndale House Publishers, a Division of Tyndale House Ministries, Carol Stream, Illinois 60188. All rights reserved.

Scripture quotations marked (NIV) are taken from the Holy Bible, New International Version®, NIV®. Copyright © 1973, 1978, 1984, 2011 by Biblica, Inc.® Used by permission of Zondervan. All rights reserved worldwide. www.zondervan.com The "NIV" and "New International Version" are trademarks registered in the United States Patent and Trademark Office by Biblica, Inc.®

ISBN: 978-1-6642-1817-8 (sc)
ISBN: 978-1-6642-1818-5 (hc)
ISBN: 978-1-6642-1816-1 (e)

Library of Congress Control Number: 2020925862

Print information available on the last page.

WestBow Press rev. date: 02/10/2021

DEDICATION

First, this is dedicated to Jesus and His prompting me to learn from everyday life. That His Spirit will take this to those that need it. That He will use it to encourage and strengthen all that read it.

Although she has contributed some tidbits to this book and is considered a co-author, I wish to also dedicate this book to my lovely and loving wife, Kathy. She was a constant inspiration and encouragement to me.

We both would like to dedicate this work to our daughters; (listed according to age) Dana, Justine, Alicia, Kristin and Carly. Their love and support of us is immeasurable.

ACKNOWLEDGMENTS

There are a few people that we would also like to acknowledge. They have encouraged us many times along this journey. They are; Bill Brack, Mary French, Bob Garraway & Betty Krottenaurer.

We would also like to thank our granddaughter, Alaina Nielsen, for taking the wonderful picture of us that is on the back cover.

CONTENTS

PERSONAL STORY TIDBITS

HOLIDAY TIDBITS

NEW YEAR TIDBITS

EASTER AND PASSOVER TIDBITS

CHRISTMAS TIDBITS

PREFACE

I feel that God showed me some time ago that I am to look at everyday life experiences and see if there is a lesson to be learned. That is what spawned me, several years ago, to begin writing, what I call, my tidbits. I found that there is so much that can be learned from everyday life and I want to share what God taught me over those years.

Although I started this as a possible devotional, that's not what it has turned out to be. There are only 95 tidbits... not 365 or 366 as you would find with a daily devotional. Plus, if it would be a daily devotional, would the devotion, that I placed on a certain day, line up with what each individual, reading this book, would need on that day? Instead, I decided to place them in such a manner that they can be read in order or at random.

You will find 5 different styles of tidbits in this book:

The first style is based on God telling me to learn from everyday experiences. The tidbits include personal stories from my life and what I've learned as a result of them. I know that these experiences aren't unique to just me. I am sure that you can apply them to experiences that you may have had in your life.

Second, I use other story lines, rather than my personal experiences, to bring home a lesson.

Third, there are also some lessons that God gave me straight from the scriptures that we are to apply to everyday life. It's not that those teachings are a revelation for mankind, as I am probably not the first to acquire that same knowledge from those scriptures. I just needed to put them in an understandable perspective… if for no one else, so that I could better understand. I decided to share them as well.

Fourth, there are 5 tidbits that my wife, Kathy, penned. They are from, specifically, her perspective and, generally, a woman's perspective. Personally, I love them all.

Fifth, although these tidbits can be considered cross-overs of the other styles, their main focus is on the various holidays that we celebrate throughout the year in the United States. I have even given some of the bigger holidays their own sections.

So, as you read, I hope you enjoy. I also hope that if there is a lesson, encouragement or even a revelation in any tidbit that may apply to you, that it will bless you!

Paul Hatalsky

PERSONAL STORY TIDBITS

This chapter has 37 tidbits. As I stated in the introduction, my main purpose for writing the tidbits was because God told me to find lessons in everyday life. It seems as though I have lived quit a few experiences and, as a result, have learned quit a few lessons.

Although they are my personal experiences, I challenge you to apply them to similar experiences that you may have had. Perhaps, one day, I will be reading your tidbits.

SIX IS ENOUGH

Judges 7:2 *The LORD said to Gideon, "The people who are with you are too many for Me to give Midian into their hands, for Israel would become boastful, saying, 'My own power has delivered me.'"*

Kathy and I have been on mission trips to El Salvador, through our church, many times. Each trip has memories, but not all have lessons like the one that we learned on our first trip there.

We were scheduled to go to a government run orphanage for boys on our third day. When a few of our people got sick the night before, plans changed. Not only did the sick remain back, but there were a couple of our people that also stayed back to care for our own.

Of the 12 missionaries on that particular trip, only six of us boarded the bus that morning to visit the orphans. Because of our limited number, we also chose not to take our puppet stage and puppets. As we pulled into the gates of the facility, horror struck the half dozen of us. Our bus was not only greeted by hundreds of children, but also an El Salvador television news crew. We found out that they were expecting the full treatment... especially puppets. We explained our dilemma to them about our ailing comrades, and they understood. We still felt horrible. We also thought that this is going to be disastrous.

We assembled in a large auditorium type of room where the children were seated. Kathy and I took the stage and did a mimed drama called,

'Jesus Wants Your Heart'. Within the drama, using both hands, we make the shape of a heart on our chest and then cup our hands and move them upwards as if giving our heart to God.

Following that, another of our team got up and, through an interpreter, gave a straight forward salvation message. He then gave an altar call. The stage was located in the front of the room and was the width of it. It was elevated about two feet above the floor. When the altar call was given, there was no room left in front of the stage as the boys of the orphanage came up and kneeled down placing their heads on the stage and praying with our brother.

The government head of orphanages was in attendance and got up after that and said some things. Our interpreter told us that she was telling the boys to thank us for coming and that they hoped our sick friends would get better. Just outside of that room was a large covered porch where we set up and passed out some refreshments, school supplies (paper, pencils, crayons, etc.), Spanish tracts and 'Gospels of John'. We had a couple of boys come up to Kathy and me and make the sign of a heart on their chest and then cup their hands towards the sky. They were telling us that they understood the drama and that they were believers. One little boy scolded Kathy because, at one point in the drama, she had broken my heart. He waved his finger at her as he told her, "No, no, no!"

What really struck me though… a little boy went to the gentleman that had given the salvation message and handed him the tract that we had given to him. Our man told him, "No. That belongs to you". The little boy pointed to the back of the tract where he had written something in Spanish and insisted that our man keep it. When we got on the bus to leave, he gave the tract to our interpreter who read what the little boy had written. It said, "Today, I gave my heart to Jesus!" There were very few dry eyes on the bus.

God told Gideon that he would only need 300 men to accomplish what needed done with the Midianites. That day at the orphanage, He told us that He only needed six to do what needed done with those precious orphans. It was so He could be glorified, not the number of people we had and not even the puppets. It was all about Him… not Gideon and not us.

Finally… don't underestimate our God. His ways are not our ways nor His thoughts ours. (Isaiah 55:8) There's a saying I once heard; 'me plus God equals a majority and with that, all things are possible'.

A PROMISE TO BUY BREAD

Colossians 3:9 – 10 *Do not lie to one another, since you laid aside the old self with its evil practices, and have put on the new self who is being renewed to a true knowledge according to the image of the One who created him*

When I was a child living in a small coal mining village in Southwestern Pennsylvania, I received some mail telling me that if I sold all occasion cards, I could earn some pretty nice prizes. I had permission from my parents to do so and I began going door to door trying to sell the cards. I actually did it on several different occasions and did earn some nice stuff… at least stuff that a 9 or 10 year old boy would have deemed nice. On one of my door to door treks, I happened upon a woman who was also going door to door. She wasn't selling… instead she was promoting products from a national bakery. She asked me what I was selling and I told her. She then made me an offer; "If you promise to buy such and such bread from now on, I'll buy a box of cards from you." Of course I wasn't going to let a chance to make a sale slip by. I promised and she bought a box of my cards. I know now that she was just a nice lady helping out a child. But, for my part, a promise was a promise. Every time that I would go shopping with my mom over the next couple of years, I would push for her to buy that brand of bread. In many instances, she would.

In Colossians 3:9, Paul says that we shouldn't lie to one another. Part of that is to not make promises that we don't keep. To do so is a lie. Paul goes on to explain why: Because "you *laid aside the old self with its evil practices…*" Do you remember your old self? Has there been a change? Are you more honest and sincere now, since coming to Christ, in the promises you make to others? ...To God?! Or, is the bottom line more important than your word!?

When I made that promise to the bread lady, I was a child and had not committed my life to Jesus. But I did strive to fulfill my promise. Why? Again, I was a child and had that childlike innocence. Jesus says, *"... Whosoever shall not receive the kingdom of God as a little child, he shall not enter therein."* (Mark 10:15). Children, unless taught or influenced to do wrong, are honest and sincere when they make a promise. Part of being renewed to a true knowledge according to the image of Christ (Colossians 3:10) is to return to those innocent childlike traits. No one would have been hurt had I broken my promise to the bread lady (That brand of bread is still on store shelves)... but, as adults, when we break promises, it could carry major consequences:

- ➤ Businesses collapse and people lose money and jobs.
- ➤ Marriages end in divorce and innocent children are scarred.
- ➤ Someone may not hear of salvation because you didn't fulfill your promise to visit them.

Put on the new self and don't lie. Be childlike and keep your promises! By the way; I can't promise that this will happen, but I do hope to, one day, see you in heaven's bread aisle.

AN ARROGANT CHURCH

Job 33:16 – 17 *Then He (God) opens the ears of men, And seals their instruction, That He may turn man aside from his conduct, And keep man from pride*

I have often said that the first church that I went to, after I was saved, taught me more about what a church should not be rather than what it should be. One example of something that I remember the pastor saying on more than one occasion, from the pulpit, was, "This is the only church in in this area where the truth is preached!" A statement like that, in my opinion, comes from a misplaced pride and arrogance. As a result, that church no longer exists.

Then there are the churches that feel that they control God. I'm not sure if that's pride or ignorance. In most cases they take scripture completely out of context and make a doctrine that is, in my opinion, offensive to our King. Examples:

- ➤ Prosperity Doctrine (Even Jesus says that we should build up treasures in Heaven, not here on earth – Matthew 6:20);
- ➤ Claiming gifts of the Spirit that <u>God</u> hasn't given to that person (I've heard of churches that try and teach people to speak in tongues – How can you teach someone to perform a gift that is

given by the Holy Spirit if the Holy Spirit hasn't given them that gift?!);

➢ Name it and claim it doctrine (Jesus said ASK (Not order) in My name and it will be given. Jesus ASKED the Father to remove the cup from Him, but ended with, *"Not My will, but Yours"* (Luke 22:42) What you ask needs to line up with God's will for you the same as it did for Jesus!)

That's not the only arrogance in today's church. Note that my references here are concerning even good Bible teaching churches with firm doctrines. We feel that we have all of the answers to solve all of the world's problems. The only correct answer for any problem is Jesus. He can solve them all… but doesn't choose to. Why? For that answer, you have to read Bible prophecy about the last days (IE: Matthew 24; Daniel; Revelation) and scriptures that talk about us having choice (IE: Joshua 24:15… *choose for yourselves today whom you will serve…*). God gives us freedoms to make choices without His interference and also has <u>His plans in motion</u> in accordance with the word that He gave His prophets… even Jesus. Yet there are times I think that we forget that. We try and tell Him what WE THINK is best or what He SHOULD/SHOULDN'T do (Not to the extreme of the church's mentioned in the previous paragraph that tries to ORDER God). At times, even when we do ask Him, we fail to end it with, "Not my will, but Yours!" Are we that much smarter than God that He needs us to tell Him how to run things? How arrogant are we!?

Not that long ago, for about 2 months, it was thought that I may have had lung cancer. Even though I knew that it could lead to death and I didn't want to die at that time because of my concern for my wife and children, I ended each prayer for life with, "Not my will, but Yours." I have to admit, that was the hardest five words I <u>ever said</u> in any of my prayers. Yet, I said them in sincerity. I'm not saying this for a pat on the back. It's just to say that even though there are times where it's very hard to face God's truth in a circumstance, we still need to turn it completely over to Him.

Let's not be so proud that it interferes with the one thing that makes us Christians… Faith (Ephesians 2:8)! God has planted the <u>true churches</u> and has given the pastors His guidance in the way that church should go so as to best instruct that congregation. If that church is boastful and proud of anything or anyone other than Jesus, then that's not of God and the pastor has failed. In Job 33:17 (the opening scripture) God wants to keep us from Pride and to allow Him to get the glory. It's for our own good and to keep us from destruction as we're told in Proverbs 16:18. Swallow your pride and let Jesus truly be in control and the Lord of your life... even if He doesn't give you everything that YOU think you are entitled to.

BEING SUBMISSIVE

---

2 Peter 2:18 *Servants, be submissive to your masters with all respect, not only to those who are good and gentle, but also to those who are unreasonable.*

No one likes being told what to do. We like being our own bosses and deciding for ourselves what to do, where to go, how something should be done… and so on and so forth. However, for a lot of us, we are under authority. Unless you're a boss or the owner of a company, there are others telling you what to do. I have experienced both sides, servant and master, at the same time.

My example: The company I worked for put me in charge of our installation department; installing 2-way radios, as well as other equipment, in both vehicles and buildings. We were fortunate to land a state contract and had to do hundreds of installs over a certain period of time for the states road department. We also still needed to maintain service for our regular clients. I was called upon to be in charge and coordinate the state jobs. I was also given the assistance of some of our technicians to help with those installs. It was important to keep on schedule so that we would meet the contractor's time schedule for completing all of the jobs. As the leader of that group of people, there were times that I had to take some disciplinary actions. In doing so, I would make sure that I gave those that I disciplined, an opportunity to correct the situation. Even though I didn't like being a disciplinarian, I was also under authority and had to be submissive to my superiors. My superiors, in turn, were under the guide lines of the contractor who, as stated above, expected us to get the work done in a timely fashion.

When you agree to work for someone, you agree with the terms presented to you. The expectations of the employer are that you will be on time and give him/her an honest day's work. If you don't than you are going against what Peter tells us to be in his second letter – the opening verse above. God instructed Peter to write those words. Notice that God isn't concerned as to whether your superiors are reasonable or not. He says that you need to be submissive. If you're not happy where you are, than seek the Lord for assistance in finding a new job. But while you are still employed at that job, if you call yourself a Christian and your co-employees know it, it's important to be a person who follows God's desires as to how you conduct yourself. If for no other reason, perhaps others, including your boss, are watching and it could bear witness to Christ in your life and perhaps also draw them to Him.

BELIEVE WHAT YOU READ

---

2 Peter 3:15b - 16 *...just as also our beloved brother Paul, according to the wisdom given him, wrote to you, as also in all his letters, speaking in them of these things, in which are some things hard to understand, which the untaught and unstable distort, as they do also the rest of the Scriptures, to their own destruction.*

My salvation testimony is pretty simple to sum up: Many people, including my mother-in-law, had witnessed to me for at least ten years. When my first marriage ended, I realized that I needed someone that would never leave me or forsake me (Hebrews 13:5 - KJV). I turned to my mother-in-law and she told me that Jesus is that someone. I accepted Him as my Lord and Savior.

As a baby Christian, and reeling from the failing of my marriage, I would read scriptures that spoke of marriage, divorce, adultery and second marriage. I had all of those scriptures memorized and knew chapter and verse within only a few months of reading the Bible. My thoughts, as a result of my readings, was that my wife needed to find Jesus and repent and then, hopefully, we would reconcile. Although that is truth, the scriptures I didn't want to dwell on were that she could still come to Jesus and be forgiven <u>even if our marriage ended</u>. Yet, that's exactly what happened. Although our marriage ended, she, one day, gave her life to Jesus and now walks in salvation. God didn't change His word on my account. His desire, all along, was for her to also come to Him. (Romans 5:8)

Quite a few years ago, I remember hearing the following statement: When you read the Bible, believe what you read… don't just read what you believe. Hearing that statement brought back the memories of how I tried to <u>wrongly</u> use the scriptures, judgmentally, against my ex-wife. I was only reading what I wanted to believe.

The pastor of the first church I attended, as a baby Christian, was extremely guilty of making scriptures support what he wanted us to believe. He would use them completely out of context so as to support his doctrinal beliefs. That's why it's also important to not take <u>someone else's</u> word or follow denominational traditions without first studying them for yourself. In my opinion, that is how false doctrines get started and then thrive… people feel that those teachers or traditions are infallible and they don't bother to test them for themselves (1 John 4:1). By the way, that first church I attended no longer exists.

Paul tells Timothy in his second letter to him to study to show yourself approved of God (2 Timothy 2:15 KJV). To RIGHTLY divide the word of truth so that you can stand one day before the Lord, unashamed, knowing that you got His word right. In the opening verse above, 2 Peter 3:15b & 16, Peter, speaking about the apostle Paul, tells of those that distorted the scriptures and Paul's letters (letters that are now a part of the Bible). The consequence of that is their own destruction.

Don't just read the scriptures but study them. To not do so and to only read them in a context that supports what you want them to say is to distort them. In order to believe what you read, it's important to understand what you are reading. It's good to have study aids: concordance; a Bible (that gives good cross references); a Bible dictionary. The fact is, in this information age, there is no reason to not be able to do an extensive study of God's word.

Of course, let's not forget prayer… asking God to reveal His truth to you in the scriptures. Yes, that truth may hurt when it doesn't support what you may want it to. But, we must trust that God's word is undeniable truth (2 Timothy 3:16 & 17 NLT).

That way, when you share your faith, you'll not be sharing false doctrines, that may not lead to your destruction, but could lead to chastisement from God. When you do get it right, and on that day that you stand before God, you'll stand approved.

BENDING AN EAR

Philippians 2:3 – 4 *Do nothing from selfishness or empty conceit, but with humility of mind regard one another as more important than yourselves; do not merely look out for your own personal interests, but also for the interests of others.*

I usually have an opportunity to fly somewhere at least once a year. On one of my flights, I noticed a person that looked a lot like a character from a 1980's sitcom. When we arrived and were waiting for our luggage to come to the carousel, I saw that person sitting by himself away from everyone. Curiosity got the better of me and I went over and said something to the affect; "You look an awful lot like that person on that sitcom." His reply was, "That could be because I am that person." Knowing that he was off alone for a reason, I then told him I hope he has a nice visit and then I left him. Not long after, I saw a woman go over to him and start talking with him. Her conversation lasted a lot longer than mine. I had gotten my luggage and was leaving and she was still pretty much bending his ear. Although it was evident to me that this man probably wanted some peace and quiet, and thus I kept my conversation short, it may not have been so evident to that woman. If it was, than she was only concerned with her own personal interests (hobnobbing with a celebrity) rather than that gentleman's interests.

We need to be aware of others feelings. The way I try and look at it; How would I like to be treated at any given time? Jesus gives us, what we call, the golden rule: *Treat others the same way you want them to treat you.* Luke 6:31

In Philippians 2:3 - 4 (above) it says that we should look out for the interests of others. But then it goes even further as to say; Regard the other as more important than yourself! The question we should ask ourselves, pertaining to that scripture, is: "Do I consider others more important?"

Let's examine that. Ask yourself the following:

1) Do I enter into conversations with people that I'm not comfortable with because of appearance or that they just don't fit the criteria of people I like associating with? (IE: They're not one of the beautiful people). More so, would I invite them to spend time with me?

2) If a friend or someone that meets my criteria asks for help, do I consider giving it? If I don't consider them a friend, only an acquaintance, and they ask for help, do they get the same consideration?

3) When I do speak with others, do I take in to consideration their feelings and what they might be going through? Or, is the conversation all about me?

4) Am I willing to share what I have, even with those that I may not consider to be close? Or like in a Daffy Duck cartoon, do I run around saying, "MINE, MINE, MINE!"

Are we called to have this extreme of humility? If you're not sure, read Philippians 2:3 & 4 again. There are many forms of humility. Putting others before you is one of God's most important ways of calling us to be humble. Remember Jesus' yoke: *"Love your neighbor as yourself"* Matthew 22:39

COLD FRENCH FRIES

Luke 6:31 (NLT) *Do to others as you would like them to do to you.*

On one of my mission trips to El Salvador, there was an evening in which our team was having dinner at a restaurant near our hotel. Seeing the nature of our trip (to help those that may not even have the guarantee of a meal that night), I was faced with a decision when I received my meal and the french fries were cold. Should I send them back to be reheated? If this were a restaurant in the states, that would be a no brainer... of course send them back. But this was El Salvador. Then it struck me; should that even matter?

This reaffirmed to me how spoiled we really are in our society (Notice, I said WE. I include myself in this mindset). If I had sent them back, it probably would have reaffirmed to the waiter and the cook (who probably were making poverty level wages), if they were told that we were missionaries from the United States, how proud and arrogant those greengo's can be. It would have also been a poor witness for Christ.

It's important to understand where you are and who you're being a witness to before over reacting about something... or even just reacting. In the U. S. where the cook would probably be making a decent wage and the waiter would like to receive a nice tip, it probably wouldn't have impacted them as much. I wonder if the roles were reversed and I would have been the waiter or cook (perhaps knowing that my children may have been eating cold beans and rice for dinner - a staple meal for a lot of

El Salvadorians who can't afford better) and the french fries would have been sent back.

In Luke 6:31 (NLT), when Jesus tells us to treat others as we would like to be treated, He doesn't put any conditions on that. He doesn't say treat others as you want to be treated unless they do something to offend you. Then it's OK to be rude and arrogant with them.

It's time to take Jesus at His word. How often we pick and choose what we want to obey and fluff off the other things thinking that Jesus understands. As God's children, He probably understands that, at times, we act like spoiled brats. That's when He has to step in and deal with us as a loving, yet disciplinary Father.

The next time you're unhappy with a situation or a person, stop and think, before you react, as to what Jesus would do. Also think of what kind of a witness you're being to others… whether they are the perpetrator(s) or those watching you (IE: maybe even your own children). But more so, think of how you would want to be treated in that situation if the roles were reversed. Then do to them as you would want them to do to you.

COMPASSION VERSES RELIGION

Matthew 9:13 *"But go and learn what this means: 'I DESIRE COMPASSION, AND NOT SACRIFICE,' for I did not come to call the righteous, but sinners."*

One of Jesus' biggest struggles was religion. In Matthew 9:11 – 12, He is once again confronted by the religious when they see Him eating with tax collectors and sinners. In Matthew 9:13 (Above) is His response. Jesus was referencing old testament scriptures that talk about compassion over religion. I feel that one scripture He may have been thinking of is, Micah 6:6, 7 and, for my point, especially Micah 6:8: *He has told you, O man, what is good; And what does the LORD require of you But to do justice, to love kindness, And to walk humbly with your God?* (To, "Love kindness", means to practice kindness).

In a breakdown of some of the words of the opening scripture: If you look at, "I desire", the Greek word used there is, 'Thelo'… which also means; to take delight in. And, if you look at the word, "compassion", the Greek word is, 'Eleos"… which also means; mercy or love.

So often we, as Christians, seem to forget that Jesus is about mankind and not being religious. His delight is for us to reach out and show kindness to others more than to be in church every time the doors open. (Not that being in church is a bad thing. But, even church needs to be prioritized.)

Example: There's a person who worked full time in a ministry that was associated with a church. One particular week, that church had an evangelist come to speak for several evenings in a row. It was during that time that the grandmother of the head of that ministry passed away. The person asked some people of that ministry if they were going to the funeral home the night that the grandmother was laid out. Their response was that they couldn't go because they needed to hear the evangelist, even though they had already heard him on other nights. The evangelist was also scheduled to be there the following night as well. At the funeral home, as the ministry head was hugging and thanking those that did attend, a grateful tear could be seen in her eyes. She needed that love and caring at that moment.

Jesus says that He takes delight in us showing love to others. Jesus also tells us of His passion when it comes to ministering to others. Beginning in Matthew 25 verse 31 He tells the parable of the sheep and goats. What the scripture is saying, condensed: In as much as you've shown those in need... love, you've shown Jesus love! Those that chose to go to the funeral home that night weren't just showing love to the ministry head... they were, in effect, showing love to Jesus.

Have you given Jesus opportunities to delight in you because of your compassion for others? If so, than keep it up and bring many smiles to our Lord. If not, it's not too late to start. You don't have to look far. A good place to start is in your church. Don't be shy about asking others what you can do to serve them. If they have a need, they'll let you know. By showing that love, you can be a delight to them and Jesus.

CONFORMED OR TRANSFORMED

Romans 12:2 *And do not be conformed to this world, but be transformed by the renewing of your mind, so that you may prove what the will of God is, that which is good and acceptable and perfect.*

Several years ago, my wife and I were invited to a wedding. The crowd was mostly made up of professing Christians. The bride and groom were also professing Christians. There were many young people there and it wasn't surprising that some modern secular music was played. What was surprising was a dance that the groom did with the bride. I'm not going to go into detail, but it was extremely sexual in nature. There was a huge crowd, including a lot of professing Christians, that stood around the dance floor cheering on the dance.

During a study tour to Israel that my wife and I took, we visited the ruins of Caesarea Philippi. This city, in Jesus' time, was steeped in pagan worship. They especially worshipped Pan... a half man, half goat god found in both Roman and Greek mythology. The city was up against a large cliff. A sizable cave at one corner of the cliff use to gush water out of it (it is now dry due to seismic activity). It was believed to be a gate to the underworld or the 'Gates of Hell'. There are many niches carved in the rock of the cliff that, at one time, held statues of Pan. There were temples built to other gods as well as Pan. There was an outside area reserved for sexual acts to be publically done to honor Pan in hopes that he would grant fertility in all aspects of the lives of those that worshipped him.

This is the place that Jesus took His disciples and asked them, *"But, who do you say that I am?"* (Matthew 16:15). Peter responded in the next verse, Matthew 16:16, by saying, *"You are the Christ, the Son of the living God."* Jesus tells Peter he has done well and that God the Father has revealed that to him. In Matthew 16:18, Jesus says that the "Gates of Hell" will not prevail against a church made up of many who have that same faith that Peter had. Peter would have understood what Jesus was saying: that the true church is made up of many stones (Matthew 16:18 - Jesus referred to Peter as a stone); these stones combined would become the massive rock (Jesus referred to the church as that rock); and that it will stand up to even the grievous example of sin as found at Caesarea Philippi.

What happened at that wedding reminded me of Caesarea Philippi. I think of how Jesus said that His church would prevail against such acts as that (NOTE: prevail means to be on the offensive = attack; not the defensive). Yet, at that reception, I felt that the gates of hell remained solid. The strong Christian witness that took place during the wedding ceremony, to the unbelievers that were present, was destroyed. The enemy held off another potential Christian victory.

There's a Biblically based Christian cliché that says we are to be in this world but not be a part of this world (reference John 15:19). As Christians, we should not give in to the world and become a part of it. Instead, we should take that opportunity to attack the gates of hell. It's time to take a stand church. It's Okay to be different and not conform to the society outside of the church. To have a celebration where God is honored instead of paying more homage to the idols of today. To be transformed to God's will.

CONTRARY SPIRIT

Galatians 5:17a (NIV) *For the flesh desires what is contrary to the Spirit, and the Spirit what is contrary to the flesh.*

There is an outdoor area in Pittsburgh called Market Square. It's an open area, about the size of a baseball field, surrounded by various shops and restaurants. On one corner of the square is a covered stage. On three Saturdays throughout the summer, my church would apply for use of the stage. We would take our worship leaders and for about two and a half hours we would play worship music, have a couple of salvation messages, give out food and supplies to the homeless and have one on one witnessing to the people that would stop to listen.

At that time I was considered the sound expert and manned the sound mixer board. Prior to our group doing some of the worship and preaching, I would play Christian music via CD's. I had freedom to choose what songs to play. On one particular outreach, I felt strongly to play, 'There Is A God', by Carman. If you're not familiar with the song; the beginning of it tells how the earth (its orbit from the sun, its axis and rotation, the atmosphere around it) was no accident but designed by God.

As I was playing the song, there were two young women standing behind me. One of them asked, in an exasperated voice; "Why are you playing that? Put something better on." I refused her request and then I had to go deal with some wiring on the stage so that it would be ready for when we started the outreach. While I was correcting the wiring, I heard the

Carman song suddenly interrupted and another upbeat, feel good song replace it. When I returned to the board, I asked my trainee why he changed the song. He told me that the girls had asked him to. Just then, the leader of the outreach came up to us and asked, "What was that song that was on before this one? The words in it are exactly what I am going to be preaching about today."

Was I in tune with what the Spirit wanted to get across that day? I like to think that I was. I believe that the Holy Spirit will put brothers and sisters on the same page. However, there are times when we give in to what <u>we</u> want and lose touch with what the Spirit may want. The two girls didn't mean any harm. And, NO, it's not that I am more spiritual than they are. However, on that particular day, they got caught up in wanting to hear something that was more 'feel good' sounding and they didn't consider the words to the song I was playing.

This is a good lesson of what we need to do on a daily basis. In the previous verse to the opening verse above; Galatians 5:16, Paul says: *But I say, walk by the Spirit, and you will not carry out the desire of the flesh.* We need to be sensitive to what the Spirit wants on a daily basis… even on a minute by minute basis. Don't let your guard down. Don't get caught up in the desires of the flesh or your senses. Let the Spirit of the Lord guide you in everything you do.

DESIRES OF THE HEART

Psalm 37:4 *Delight yourself in the Lord; And He will give you the desires of your heart.*

MY DESIRES:

When I was about 10 years old, I received a tape recorder for Christmas. It was a small, inexpensive reel to reel. The following summer, my friend and I used it to play 'disc jockey' on my front porch. When I reached junior high school, one of my teachers asked my class to choose what we would like to be when we grew up. One choice was to be a radio disc jockey… I put a check mark beside it.

Move forward in time to my mid-twenties. I had always loved the sound of bass in music. One day I was visiting my brother-in-law and he showed me his bass guitar. It was then that I had a desire to want to learn to play it. Time and finances stood in my way during that period of my life.

Move forward to my early thirties. My first wife had left me. (It was that event that brought me to Jesus.) At first, I had hoped for reconciliation. After that I wanted to focus on my daughters. As my daughters grew and became more independent, it was then that I had a desire to be married again.

<u>MY RESULTS</u>:

Three years after coming to Christ, I took my mom to visit her sister in West Virginia. While there, I heard a Christian radio station advertising for volunteer DJ's. I put my application in. I was accepted on the spot and for the next 10 years was an on-air personality at the station.

Eight years after starting at the radio station, I was in a local music store with my oldest daughter. Because of an injury to my left hand, that restricts the movement of my index finger, I was interested in learning to play a left handed bass. I was unsuccessful in finding a 'Lefty' in any store until that day. The music store had 2 and one was in my favorite color… green! I asked my daughter her thoughts about me buying it. Her answer; "Dad, you've wanted to play for a long time… why not now?" I bought the guitar. Less than 2 years later, I was playing on our worship band at church.

Sometime within my first year of playing the bass, I noticed that a girl, which I had not seen before, began attending the Wednesday evening services. I found out later that she also noticed me on the stage. We eventually were introduced and ten and a half months later, we were married.

The Lord granted me those desires of my heart. But, notice, especially with becoming a DJ and playing the bass; it wasn't until I gave my life to Jesus that they were granted and they were/are being used to glorify Him. My desires for a wife came after I was a Christian, and God has blessed me with a very Godly woman. I remember asking the Lord for specific characteristics in a future wife (But I always finished that prayer with, "Lord; Your will be done!"). I am blessed that my wife has every one of those traits that I prayed for.

As Psalm 37:4 says, we are to delight ourselves in the Lord. If there are desires that you have, first delight yourself in the Lord. Then, ask the Lord if what you want is what He wants for you. It's OK if He says no. Take delight in that and move forward knowing that His plans for you are better. (Jeremiah 29:11)

FRUSTRATIONS

Ecclesiastes 5:17 (NLT) *Throughout their lives, they live under a cloud—frustrated, discouraged, and angry.*

Not long ago, my year started out typical to most previous years. There were no surprises or concerns other than the normal things of everyday life. I had helped some friends by doing some electrical wiring in their house. I also went to El Salvador on a very rewarding mission's trip. But then, around mid-march, I got very ill. I ran a fever for several days and had little to no energy. I went to my doctor who ordered several tests, including a chest x-ray. When the results of the x-ray came back, they had noticed something on my right lung. I then went for a CT scan. When those results came back, the initial diagnosis was pneumonia. I was given antibiotics and told to get a follow up CT scan in a month. When I did, the 'thing' on my lung was still there and hadn't shrunk. Now the concern turned to cancer. I went for a pet scan and then a biopsy... all of which seemed to take forever to get the results back. Finally, on May 31st of that year, I went to my pulmonary doctor and was told that it was not cancer. Instead, it was caused by a fungal infection. I was put on an anti-fungal medication and the 'thing' in my lung began to shrink. My thanking of the Lord was quit intense as you may imagine.

My health problems didn't end there though. I have had a problem with acid reflux and a little over a month later, I had a major flare up. This combined with times of seeing some blood in my phlegm sent me, once again, to my doctor. It turned out that the blood was coming more from my nasal cavity due to dryness from being in a lot of air conditioning. However, the acid reflux was with me for the remainder of the year.

This was a very frustrating time for me and my wife (who I thank God daily for her and her love and devotion to me). King Solomon tells us, in the book of Ecclesiastes 5:10 – 17 (NLT), that there will be frustration, discouragement and even anger in this life. But then, in Ecclesiastes 5:18 through 20 (NLT), he says this: *Even so, I have noticed one thing, at least, that is good. It is good for people to eat, drink, and enjoy their work under the sun during the short life God has given them, and to accept their lot in life. And it is a good thing to receive wealth from God and the good health to enjoy it. To enjoy your work and accept your lot in life—this is indeed a gift from God. God keeps such people so busy enjoying life that they take no time to brood over the past.*

Here's my take on those verses: God wants us to enjoy life including our work; Life is short; It's good when things are going well and we receive good things, but we should also be joyful and accept our lot in life; God gives joy as a gift; If we keep busy with what God has for us, we will find joy and won't have time to be frustrated over the sad and bad things that we may have to go through. (Read John 16:33)

We don't know what the coming year may bring to us. It may be all good… it may be all bad… it may be a mixture of good and bad. Whatever happens though, find joy and peace in the Lord. Joy in the fact that, if you are a Christian, you belong to Him and no matter what, He's in control. I can tell you from personal experience that it is very difficult to pray, "Lord, Your will be done!", when you aren't sure what His will is. But that is where faith and trust come in. Let that be your joy when nothing else seems to help. Set your mind on the fact that He lives in you through His Holy Spirit. 1 Chronicles 16:27 *Splendor and majesty are before Him, Strength and joy are in His place (YOU).*

IN SICKNESS AND IN HEALTH

Ephesians 5:31 *For this reason a man shall leave his father and mother and shall be joined to his wife, and the two shall become one flesh.*

As I indicated in the previous tidbit, I had a very trying year physically. There was a fear that I had lung cancer (which turned out to be a fungal infection). Then, my acid reflux, which I've had for several years, decided, during that same year, to flare up and become a constant nuisance. I developed a cold late in the year and that caused me to contract a sinus infection (complete with blood in my mucus). All of this meant many doctors and hospital visits. It also meant, even with health insurance, paying co-pays and deductibles that totaled a few thousand dollars.

Through all of that, there was my wife by my side. She went to my doctor's visits with me and spent a lot of time in the hospital during my CT scans and biopsies. She was patient during my days where I lacked any energy to do anything and never complained once about how much money we had to shell out for medical expenses.

In most Christian marriage ceremonies, the following words are uttered by both the bride and the groom: "Do you, (the name of the bride or the groom) promise to love, honor and cherish (the name of the other person) for better; for worse; for richer; for poorer; in sickness and in health, til death do you part?" These vows mean that a marriage is to last through thick and thin.

Ephesians 5:31 (above) tells us that when we are married, we become one with that other person. We are no longer two people, but one. Ephesians 5:28 and 29 are a confirmation of becoming one. The verses say that husbands should love their wives as their own bodies. That if you love your wife, than you love yourself. As a result, the scripture says that we want to take care of ourselves and thus would want to take care of our spouse. For that reason, when one of you is going through a hard time... you both share in it. If one of you is sick, you both suffer the illness. You are one!

Too often the promises that are made in a wedding vow are forgotten. One person in the relationship can't deal with the others problem and chooses to end the relationship (Even if they stay together, they wind up just living in the same house and nothing more). The oneness is gone. It's like separating, in a spiritual sense, Siamese twins. That's not what God wants. He wants us to remain one with each other. We're to support each other regardless of the circumstances. To treat our spouse as we would want to be treated. After all, according to scripture in more places than just Ephesians 5:31, we are one... our spouse is a part of us!

Ephesians 5:29 also says that it's the same as how Christ cherishes the church and how we, since we are a part of the church, are one with Him. How big of a comparison is that!? In Ecclesiastes 4:12, it says that a cord of three strands is not easily broken. In marriage those strands are you, your spouse and Jesus... all wrapped together as one. Don't allow anything, in your life together, cause you to even try and break that cord... Not bad times; not finances; not sickness... NOTHING!

KEEPING THE CAT WARM

Matthew 10:29 - *"Are not two sparrows sold for a cent? And yet not one of them will fall to the ground apart from your Father."*

Several years back, a beautiful tortoiseshell cat began appearing at our house. Normally, I would chase a stray away, but for some reason I allowed this cat to keep coming. It turns out that this was, sort of, a neighborhood cat. Most of our neighbors would put some food out for her but there was one neighbor lady that seemed to claim the responsibility for her. She took on the expense of taking Mama Cat to a vet to get her necessary shots and to be spayed. This was after Mama had a litter of kittens (which, by the way, were given away – & thus the reason that we call her Mama Cat). She hated being indoors though. So, she remained outside and a roamer of the neighborhood.

At first she was very skittish around my wife and me. I would put my hand out towards her, in a non-threatening way, and eventually, I was able to touch her. After some time, I was petting her and then was able to pick her up. That first winter, on a sub-zero night, I tried to put her in our basement. She would have nothing to do with it. She stood by the door that led to the outside and meowed rather loudly until I let her out.

The neighbor lady, that had claimed her and took on the caring responsibilities, had to move away and couldn't take the cat with her. Since Mama was comfortable with my wife and me, she asked us to take on the responsibilities of the cat's care. We agreed and we would buy food and have a shelter, with blankets in it, on the porch for her. She became so comfortable with us, she would jump up on our laps when we were sitting on the porch.

There was one winter that was rather brutal. The temperature dipped well below zero degrees Fahrenheit on several occasions. I couldn't stand to think of Mama being out in that kind of cold. I made a bed in the basement for her and bought a disposable litter box. I enticed her to come into the house and then took her to the basement. This time I ignored her pleas to be put back outside and didn't release her until morning. She protested again the second time I took her in, but, by the third time, when I would open the back door for her to come in, she headed straight to the basement. For the remainder of the winter, when the temperature would dip too low, Mama would spend the night in our basement. She learned that I was trying to help her, not imprison her.

How often do we do that with God? He offers us a better set of circumstances to help us and, in some cases, protect us, and we don't accept it. We think we know what's best even when He tries to make it clear that He has us covered. We seem to forget His promise to us that's found in Jeremiah 29:11 'For I know the plans that I have for you,' declares the LORD, 'plans for welfare and not for calamity to give you a future and a hope.'

When we finally do give in to His wishes, we find that things would have been better all along had we just trusted Him at first (The same way Mama Cat discovered that a warm basement on a cold night was pretty comfy).

God knows us better than we know ourselves. He created us in our mother's womb (Psalm 139:13). We need to not argue with Him, the way Mama Cat argued with me the first time I put her in the basement. Instead, trust that He is doing what is best for you. Let's not trust in our own understanding, but rather seek the Lord's guidance and then follow it.

If He is concerned about a sparrow falling to the ground, how much more is His concern for us.

LEFT HANDED BASS PLAYER

Ephesians 5:1 *Therefore be imitators of God, as beloved children*

My wife and I have been to Walt Disney World in Florida several times. We enjoy going to EPCOT and visiting the World Showcase. For those of you who have not been there; the World Showcase is a large portion of EPCOT where different countries from throughout the world are represented. Each country has some type of structure and even a mockup of something iconic from that country. For example: France has a miniature Eiffel Tower. They all have some type of attraction… a show; a ride; a restaurant that serves traditional food from that country.

On one particular trip, as we were strolling past the England pavilion, there was a band playing Beatle's music in an adjacent gazebo. Since there were 4 musicians and they were dressed sort of sixtyish, we assumed that they were imitating the Beatles.

I play bass guitar and I play it left handed. I have gone up to different musicians that I have seen at concerts and made the statement (In as good of a British accent as I can – which isn't that good): "My name is Paul and I play a left handed bass." (FYI: <u>Paul</u> McCartney, of the Beatles, plays a left handed bass.) Sometimes they get it (as musician/singer Paul Baloche did) and sometimes they don't.

After the Beatle imitators were done playing, they made themselves available for the audience to have their picture taken with them. I waited my turn and then went up to the bass player and I gave my line. I am pretty sure that he was clueless as to what I was referring to when his response was to ask me if I wanted to take his place.

Here is a person that was supposed to be imitating someone, but, in reality, it was questionable as to how much he really knew about that person.

How often are we like that with God!?

First, are we really imitators as Paul said that we should be in Ephesians 5:1 (Above)? Or are we just going through the motions of everyday living rather than the pursuit of doing God's will in our life? Are we so caught up in desiring His miracles, healings, blessings that we forget that we need to also do our part?

Second, are we doing everything we can to learn more about our God and to understand Him so that we can better imitate Him?

In I Corinthians 11:1, Paul says; *"Be imitators of me, just as I also am of Christ."* It's important to understand that when the original letters were written, they weren't divided into chapter and verse. If you look at 1 Corinthians 10, you can see the ways of imitating that Paul is referring to. One way is in 1 Corinthians 10:33. Paul says; *"just as I also please all men in all things, not seeking my own profit but the profit of the many, so that they may be saved."*

Part of being an imitator of Christ is to be unselfish. To be more concerned about the Spiritual gain of those around us rather than the Natural gain that we could receive from Him. After all, Jesus, desiring our salvation, gave up <u>everything </u>for us. That's just one of many examples of what we can learn so as to better imitate Him.

Study the scriptures, as Paul instructs in 2 Timothy 2:15 (KJV), and then be an imitator of our God.

MISSION: TO BE DIVIDENDS

Mark 16:15 - *And He said to them, "Go into all the world and preach the gospel to all creation".*

I make mention in other tidbits, that my wife and I went to Egypt, Jordan and Israel on a teaching tour. The one thing that our teacher kept telling us is that we are not tourists… we are investments. In short, by us studying God's word in depth, that is God's way of making an investment in us.

For several years, around mid-February, my wife and I have traveled to El Salvador, Central America, doing missions work. This started when a woman that attends our church, originally born in El Salvador, approached our senior pastor and told him of a need to care for the orphans in that country. Our senior pastor sent a small exploratory group to El Salvador to scope out the situation. As a result of that trip, the Holy Spirit quickened to our leadership that our church needed to be missionaries to the children and people of that small country.

On one of the trips, I felt to share from 1 Corinthians 15:58 - *Therefore, my beloved brethren, be steadfast, immovable, always abounding in the work of the Lord, knowing that your toil is not in vain in the Lord.* After reading that verse, I explained what our teacher had said to us on our trip to the Middle East about being investments and not tourists. I then explained that on this trip, a mission trip where we are giving out what has already been invested in us, we are not tourists nor investments. Instead, we are to bring forth the dividends that are a result of those investments.

You have been invested in also. When!? When you hear a message preached or taught at church or on the radio or on TV; when you study your Bible and pray for understanding of the Word; when God speaks to you through your spouse or a friend; when you pray and God speaks directly to you in your spirit. Those are all investments that God is making in you and from them He wants you to bring forth dividends.

Look at it this way: you can only fit so much liquid in a jar without it overflowing and some of the liquid being wasted. So you need to empty some out into other vessels before adding more. God wants to invest in you more and more but He doesn't want it to go to waste. He wants you to take what He's invested in you and invest it in others so as to make even more investments and yield even more dividends.

I think of Matthew 25:14 – 30 concerning the two slaves increasing the talents that were entrusted to them. (For the purpose of my point here, I am not going to comment on the one slave that didn't produce an increase of what was given him… but, consider his fate when you read those verses). There are different interpretations that can be made in respect to those verses: from using our spiritual gifts wisely to even using our earthly possessions to glorify the Lord and thus gain an increase. I like to apply those verses, and I don't feel wrongly so, thusly: taking the knowledge that God has invested in us and bringing an increase of souls by sharing that knowledge with others and thus drawing them closer to God (and even salvations) as a result.

Therefore, as it says in 1 Corinthians 15:58, *our toil is not in vain*. Even though we may not see immediate results when doing the work of the Lord… if we do our part, God will be faithful in doing His part and yielding the dividends.

Final thought: the opening scripture for this day is Mark 16:15. It says go into ALL the world and preach the Gospel. I know that not everyone reading this will have the resources to go to a foreign country. Because of your circumstances, you may not even be able to leave you own home. But, where ever you are and how ever far you can travel, isn't that part of 'the world'. There is no reason that you can't be producing dividends right where you're at.

MR. LONELY

Ecclesiastes 7:8 *The end of a matter is better than its beginning; Patience of spirit is better than haughtiness of spirit.*

Before meeting my wife, Kathy, I was always up for a road trip with friends. One such road trip happened on one cold and snowy March day. A group of us decided to go to a Christian concert that was about a 2 ½ hour drive from us. Nine of us took to the road on that cold, snowy day.

The trip there was filled with some anxious moments due to slippery roads and slow moving trucks… but, we made it safely. The concert was great and getting to meet and hang out with the artists after was a memorable experience. However, even more of a memory, that brought me to a reality in my own life, was a conversation I had, on the way back, with one of my co-travelers. We'll call him, Mr. Lonely.

Mr. Lonely was never married. Being a Christian, he remained celibate. Although he had dated and entered into a couple of semi-serious relationships, it just never worked out for him to take that next step – marriage. He opened up to me about his deep desire to be married and couldn't understand why he wasn't. As we talked, I told him that we needed to be patient and wait on God. His reply was that he has been patient, but God isn't doing anything about it. In short, he was growing impatient and wanted to take matters into his own hands.

I have to admit, at that time, even though I was being the voice of reason to him, I was struggling with the same desire. Our conversation that evening got me to do some serious thinking about my true feelings concerning my singleness. I was constantly praying for a spouse. I would add the pat Christian answer at the end of those prayers; "Your will, not mine". But, was I sincere? After asking that question, I then prayed again… but this time making sure of my sincerity (Not exact words… but probably pretty close):

> Father… You know the desire of my heart is to be married. I miss that companionship and want to share my life with someone special. I would love to be able to hold the hand of that special person while we worship You together. But, Lord, I know that Your plans for my life may mean that I should remain single. If that's so, then remove the desire I have. I now realize that if that is what You want for me, then that is what will be best and I am OK with that. I'm willing to remain single. Your will be done Lord.

When I prayed that, I prayed it with full understanding of what I was saying. I knew that by saying those words, I may be closing the door on ever being married again. But I also knew that He would help me through it and use me in my singleness. I needed to be patient and wait on Him to do what was right for me in my life. I needed to not be self-indulgent or haughty in spirit and take matters in my own hands. My testimony from that is that once I let go and let Him, it wasn't long after that, that I was blessed with Kathy. There is no doubt in either of our minds that our relationship is truly of Him. The end is definitely better than the beginning.

MY (SPIRITUAL) BIRTHDAY

John 3:7 *"Do not be amazed that I said to you, 'You must be born again.'"*

For ten years people had been telling me about Jesus. I went to church and I led a good life. I did more good than bad. As far as I was concerned, I knew who Jesus was and I was going to heaven. Man was I wrong!

I was in to religion and wasn't given the truth about salvation. It was all about works. If I am good, confess my sins, go to church all the time, take communion often and if I completed all of the churches requirements, then I may make it into heaven if people pray for me once I die. None of that can save us! Salvation is by Jesus Christ alone and not by any of our works (Ephesians 2:8 – 9). Works are a result of our salvation, not to earn it. Note: My goal is not to bash any denomination… I am just passing on God's truth, through the Bible, about salvation.

I now know different and it took my first marriage coming to an end to get my attention. On one August 3rd, the reality that my marriage was over hit me and I was devastated (I have often commented that I wouldn't wish that type of pain on my worst enemy). After contemplating what to do, those ten years of being witnessed to flooded my mind. I knew that I needed this Jesus that I was told would <u>never leave me</u>. The next day (August 4th), I went to my mother-in-law (one of the Christians that had been witnessing to me and has since gone to be with the Lord). After crying out to her, she led me to Jesus. That's why I call August 4th my birthday... because it is my spiritual birthday when I, as Jesus said that we must do in the opening verse, John 3:7, was born again.

How about you? If you're reading this, chances are you probably have that personal walk with Jesus. You know what repentance is and you call Him your Lord and Savior. If not, then let today be your spiritual birthday. It's never too late to receive Jesus as your savior.

How? Simple...

> Acknowledge that you are a sinner (Romans 3:23 *for all have sinned and fall short of the glory of God*).
> Repent or desire to turn away from your sins (2 Peter 3:9b *The Lord... is patient toward you, not wishing for any to perish but for all to come to repentance.*)
> Acknowledge the deity of Jesus and what He did for you on the cross (Acts 10:36 *The word which He sent to the sons of Israel, preaching peace through Jesus Christ (He is Lord of all)*)(1 Peter 3:18 *For Christ also died for sins once for all, the just for the unjust, so that He might bring us to God, having been put to death in the flesh, but made alive in the spirit*).
> Ask Him to be your Lord and to send His Spirit to live in you (John 14:16 – 18 - In short, Jesus said: *The Father will send you the Holy Spirit. I will come to you.*) Know that there is nothing that you've done to keep you from God's love (Romans 5:8 *But God demonstrates His own love toward us, in that while we were yet sinners, Christ died for us*).

At the time I am writing this, I have walked with the Lord for 30+ years. There have been ups and downs during that time. But, my faith has not waivered. God's grace is sufficient for all (2 Corinthians 12:9). Our part – just have faith (Ephesians 2:8 – 9) and to love Him (Jude 1:21).

One last thing: if you did make today your birthday, there is a birthday celebration going on in heaven right now. (Luke 15:10)

PERCEIVE TO RECEIVE

Matthew 10:40 *"He who receives you receives Me, and he who receives Me receives Him who sent Me."*

I have had various experiences with representatives of different "Religious Groups" coming to my door and trying to evangelize me. They are all very friendly and, for the most part, are sincere in their beliefs. They are, however, trying to sell me on the wrong Jesus. (2 Corinthians 11:3 – 4)

So how should we act when someone comes to our door and tries to sell us on another Jesus? Here are two personal examples… one showing the correct way and one showing the not so correct way.

As a young Christian, I answered a knock on my door and greeted a husband and wife team. I invited them in. The man did most of the speaking and he asked me if I knew God. After joyfully conveying that I am a Christian, I then asked what religious organization he was representing. His answer was the Jehovah Witness'. We then got into a discussion concerning various scriptures. There was no shouting or arguing. As he would wrongly quote a scripture, the Holy Spirit would quicken to me what the scripture actually said and I would correct him. To me, this in itself was a miracle. As I stated, I was a very young Christian and I had, and still have, a very poor memory. As our conversation got deeper and deeper, I felt as though I was making a breakthrough with him. His wife, on the other hand, started tugging at his arm saying, "let's go". We finally ended by me asking if I could pray and he, reluctantly, agreed (after all, he was in my house). My prayer was that the Lord would reveal the truth to which ever one of us was wrong. I don't know whatever happened to this couple but I hope that what I said got them thinking and that they eventually have given their lives to the Lord.

My second example didn't go quite as well. Once again, there was a knock on my door. This time, it was two well-dressed men. Instead of inviting them in, I went out onto the porch with them and immediately asked what religious organization that they represented. The Mormon's was their reply. I then, in a not too polite voice, started accusing them of believing all of the false doctrines that I had ever heard concerning the Mormon faith. They were taken back some but, in a much more 'Christian' way, responded by telling me that some of the doctrines I mentioned are rumors and not what they believe at all. The defenses had already gone up on both sides and the spirit of contention was already there. It was too late to try and recover and we parted company in disagreement.

In the opening verse, Matthew 10:40, Jesus says that anyone who receives me will receive Christ. In my first example, because of my way of approaching that couple, at least the husband accepted me and what I was saying. There is some hope that they may have gone on to accept the true Christ in their lives. But, in my second example; let's just say if either of those two young men got saved, it wasn't because of me… and that's sad.

Whether we are dealing with people that are into false religions, false doctrines or even if they are atheists, it's important to show them Christ. Sometimes, it is just in the way we carry ourselves. I like a quote from Saint Francis of Assisi; "Preach the Gospel at all times and when necessary, use words." Realize that if they can receive you, even by just observing how you carry yourself, then there is a possibility that a door will be opened and you can then share God's salvation with them.

PERSISTENT CATERPILLAR

Luke 11:9 *So I say to you, ask, and it will be given to you; seek, and you will find; knock, and it will be opened to you.*

The double steel doors to the church office needed painted and I was elected to do the job. It was a nice fall day and I had the doors propped open. As I was painting, I noticed a "wooly" caterpillar trying to crawl across the threshold and into the church. (NOTE: I'm not sure what their actual name is, but, they are the brown and black fuzzy caterpillars that you see in the fall.) I reached down and scooped the little creature up and took it out to the edge of the curb by the parking lot (about 15 feet away) and set it on the ground. I then went back to the door and painting. Not too much time had passed when I happened to look down at the ground and once again saw the caterpillar heading toward the open doorway. I put down my paint brush and once again, scooped it up. This time, I took it to a mulch area to the side of the entrance way (about 20 feet away), assuming that perhaps it would be more comfortable there on a natural surface rather than on concrete. Some time had passed and, to my amazement, there it was again. This time I saw it about 5 feet down the sidewalk making a beeline toward the door. For its own good and safety, this time I placed it in a grassy area under a tree about a hundred feet away. I didn't see it again.

The persistence of that little guy had to be commended. In contemplating that incident, I started thinking,' am I that persistent with God?' In the opening verse, Luke 11:9, Jesus is saying that we should seek God for answers, miracles, decisions in our lives. I think that we underplay that verse though.

Here are some definitions of the key words in the verse:

Ask in the Greek = _aiteō_ = to ask, crave, beg, desire
Seek in the Greek = _zēteō_ = to seek in order to find; to demand something
Knock in the Greek = _krouō_ = to knock (Persistently)

We're not to be wimpy or backward in our approach to God. When you ask, it's okay to beg. When you seek, it's okay to demand (Not ordering God but letting Him know it's important to you). When you knock, it's okay to be persistent.

In Luke 18:2 – 5, Jesus tells of a widow, needing legal protection, who keeps bothering an unrighteous judge. Although he denied her often, eventually he said; _"Even though I do not fear God nor respect man, yet because this widow bothers me, I will give her legal protection, otherwise by continually coming she will wear me out."_ Luke gives the reason for this parable in Luke 18:1, _Now He (Jesus) was telling them a parable to show that at all times they ought to pray and not to lose heart._

Jesus, goes even deeper in why He shared this with us: And the Lord said, _"Hear what the unrighteous judge said; now, will not God bring about justice for His elect who cry to Him day and night, and will He delay long over them? "I tell you that He will bring about justice for them quickly"._ Luke 18:6 – 8a God wants to answer our requests! He wants us to find Him! He hears our knocking!

Be like the persistent widow. Be bold when you go to God. Jesus tells us to do just that in Luke 11:9. However, also understand that God is in control… not us. There are times He must say, "No!" The Father even told Jesus, His son, 'no' when Jesus prayed to have the cup removed from Him. But following that request is something Jesus said, and we should all say in sincerity at the end of our prayers; _"Yet not as I will, but as You will."_ (Matthew 26:39)

Finally, there is one thing that is a concern to Jesus (He wouldn't have asked otherwise). In Luke 18:8b Jesus says: *"However, when the Son of Man comes, <u>will He find faith on the earth</u>?"* Taking that in the context of the parable He just told, He is wondering if when He makes His return, will those on earth still be seeking God fervently: believing that he will answer; believing He will give; believing He will open? If Jesus would return tomorrow, let you and me show Him that, 'Yes, there is still faith on the earth'. Let's be persistent caterpillars!

PETTING A MOTH (OR WAS IT A BUTTERFLY?)

1 John 4:16 – *We have come to know and have believed the love which God has for us. God is love, and the one who abides in love abides in God, and God abides in him.*

One of my responsibilities, when I worked at the church, was to change the letters of the marquee' to reflect the title of the up and coming Sunday message. On one particular warm summer Friday afternoon, I grabbed the letters for the next title and headed to the marquee' at the end of the driveway. On approaching the marquee', I saw a beautiful yellow and purple insect at the center of the base of the marquee' looking straight up as if it were reading the previous weeks title. I slowly approached it and then, using the back of my pointer finger on my right hand, reached out and gently stroked its back. At first touch, it flinched, but then allowed me to stroke it several times without batting an antenna. I then opened the front panel of the marquee' and inserted the new title. After closing the panel, I once again reached down and gently petted the tiny creature. It knew that it had nothing to fear from me.

When I told my wife Kathy about the event, she said; "Put it before the Lord to see what lesson He would want to teach you."

As I contemplated the experience over the next several days, it was curiosity, and not so much a teaching, that had me searching. It was the World Wide Web that I was searching to find out what type of insect allowed me to touch it; was it a moth or a butterfly? I typed in the best description I could and followed several web sites until I finally saw a likeness of it. It was an Imperial Moth.

As time passed, I would remember the incident but didn't dwell on it too much. About a month and a half later, it came back to mind. I reread the notes that I jotted down of the experience and asked the Lord, "What can I learn from this?"

I decided to look up the definition of 'Imperial' in the Merriam-Webster on line dictionary.

One definition was: "Of superior or unusual size or excellence". I thought of how big the moth looked compared to other moths but how small it was compared to me. I could have easily crushed it with my foot but instead showed it kindness and compassion. Isn't that the way it is with our Father. We feel so big and excellent at times, but compared to God… He could easily crush us when we do wrong. Instead, He forgives and then still shows us kindness and compassion.

Another definition was: "a member of the Imperial Family". If we have received Christ, than we are members of the Imperial family of God. Galatians 3:29 - *And if you belong to Christ, then you are Abraham's descendants, heirs according to promise.*

The difference between God and us as opposed to me and the moth was summed up in the message title that I put on the marquee' that day: "A God of Emotions". My kindness to the moth was due to a fascination that it would allow me to pet it. Our God's kindness to us is out of His emotion of pure love for us. His only desire is for us to love Him back. 1 John 4:19 – *We love, because He first loved us.*

It doesn't even matter to God whether we're a moth or a butterfly. Either way, because of His love for us, we are beautiful to Him.

THE PRAYERS OF A RIGHTEOUS MAN

James 5:16 Therefore, confess your sins to one another, and pray for one another so that you may be healed. The effective prayer of a righteous man can accomplish much.

Two weeks after Kathy and I met, we went to a local chain restaurant after the Wednesday night church service. We ate and chatted for a long time. During our conversation Kathy told me that she was going to fly to Florida, the next day, to visit her favorite Aunt and Uncle. She also explained that her uncle was sick. When it was time to leave, I walked her out to her car. It was a chilly night, but as she sat in the driver's seat, I told her that I wanted to pray for her. She had no problem with that and I prayed for her safety, her visit and for her sick uncle. She told me months later that that was when she knew that she wanted to be my wife. She said that she cried all the way home and thanked the Lord for introducing her to a man that would pray for her.

What Kathy didn't know was that I was praying for her long before we were ever introduced. Kathy and I both came out of failed marriages. When we met, she had been single for 14 years and I for 13. Following my divorce, my main interest was being a father to my daughters. It wasn't until they were in their mid-teens, and them wanting to hang out with their friends, that I began desiring companionship again.

I prayed for God to pair me with someone. I even prayed for specifics...
ie: someone that loved the Lord as much as I do; someone that I would
be attracted to in all aspects of her life (physically, mentally, spiritually);
someone that would be attracted to me and accept me for who I was. After
praying for a long time like that, it then struck me... perhaps God wanted
me to remain single like the Apostle Paul. Paul even says that remaining
single is better (1 Corinthians 7:8 & 7:32 – 34). It was then that I prayed,
"Lord, you know the desire of my heart is to have a wife. If that's not Your
will and it would be better for me to remain single and serve You... then
Your will be done!" That was in the spring. I met Kathy in November of
that same year.

Kathy embodies all of the specifics that I prayed for. We both know that
God was the author of our story together. I know that God answered my
prayers and went above and beyond my expectations.

God also answered my prayers for Kathy's safe trip and her visit to Florida
on that chilly November night. However, her uncle passed away several
months later. He was supposed to walk Kathy down the aisle at our
wedding but never made it. I never met him but, listening to Kathy's
praises about him, I wish that I had. Even with that, I feel that God
answered the prayer for her uncle also. I always end my prayers, "But
Lord, Your will be done!" His will was to take her uncle home.

God hears your prayers also. In the opening verse, James 5:16, above, the
word effective means to put forth power. What it is saying: there is power
in the prayers of the righteous. Perhaps you feel that you're not righteous
enough... truth is, you're not (and neither am I – Romans 3:10 &21 – 24).
But, if you are a believer, than you have Jesus' righteousness and power
in prayer because of Him. But, if you call Jesus Lord, then it's important
that you acknowledge that He is in control, not you. That's called faith!
You're saying, "Lord, I trust You and Your love for me and that You're
going to do what's best!"

PRIDE AND PATIENCE

Colossians 3:12 *So, as those who have been chosen of God, holy and beloved, put on a heart of compassion, kindness, humility, gentleness and patience*

I know many people that struggle with patience. It would be very easy for me to pull an example from one of them, but, I found that we need to look in a mirror first and then point the finger.

We have a slight problem in my neighborhood with people blocking public thruways (Mainly alley's, but sometimes side streets also). It got to the point that my wife and I get very frustrated because the alley where our garage is, is one of the most frequently abused.

I had just picked up my two nieces, in my pick-up truck, and we were heading to my house. I decided that I wanted to park on the street in front of the house and swung around an alley way so that I would be heading in the proper direction. Upon turning down that alley, I noticed another pick-up truck blocking the alley. Although this wasn't the alley where my garage is located, it was still very annoying to me.

With that said, it would have been very easy for me to make an extra turn down another alley and wind up not much further away from where I was going. Instead, I laid on my horn. "Who are they that they should block a public roadway?" I thought. The driver of the truck came out of a nearby garage, turned and said something to another person in the garage and then got in his truck and pulled up toward me. I had left room for him to turn into the adjoining alley, but instead, he stopped and sat there looking at me. It probably wasn't for as long as it seemed but eventually I flinched and made the turn into the other alley. When I did, I hadn't noticed that in the corner of the yard that sat at the intersection of both alleys, the land owner had put a steel beam firmly in the ground. It was low enough that I couldn't see it and, you probably guessed it; I side swiped it with my truck leaving a nice scratch and dent just in front of my right rear wheel well. As I looked in my rear view mirror, I noticed that the driver of the other truck was pulling a trailer and there was no place for him to park and no way that he could have made the turn into the other alley.

My impatience had gotten the best of me. I watched the driver in my mirror as he went by. I know that he had to have seen that I hit the post, but, I didn't see him laughing; grumbling or saying anything (like maybe calling me names); or giving any type of indecent gesture. He just kept driving. I, on the other hand, felt convicted.

Proverbs 11:2a says; *When pride comes, then comes dishonor...* even though the other driver didn't express it, my impatience undoubtedly caused me dishonor in his eyes and probably to my two nieces also.

So, what should have happened? The second part of that Proverb 11:2b says; *But with the humble is wisdom.* Had I humbled myself in the beginning and just turned down another alley, my truck wouldn't have had the dent in it. The Lord taught me that day to be patient and that it's OK to swallow some pride, even in frustration, and be humble.

PROPOSING

---

1 Corinthians 11:25 *In the same way He took the cup also after supper, saying, "This cup is the new covenant in My blood; do this, as often as you drink it, in remembrance of Me."*

After meeting, since Kathy and I were older, we knew pretty quickly that God was blessing us with each other. We had met in November and by April I was ready to ask for her hand. I wanted it to be special and decided to propose in the exact same spot that we had met several months earlier. I had the evening all planned out to surprise her. We started with dinner at a chain restaurant that we both really like. We then went to see an off-Broadway production of Beauty and the Beast (Kathy's favorite Disney animated movie). Since I had met her in the vestibule at church, that's where we were going next.

The way I talked her into stopping at the church; our men's retreat was being held at a camp that was about an hour's drive away. Kathy knew that I decided not to go that evening because I had promised to take her to the play. Instead, I was going to go the next morning. I purposely left my bass guitar at the church and told her that I had forgotten it (Yes… I lied. I've since repented). I told her that I needed to stop and get it because I was playing the next day at the retreat (that was the truth).

I had another problem though… My bass was on the stage and I had hidden her engagement ring in the vestibule of the church. How was I to get her back there? She gave me the answer as we were driving to the church. She asked if I had directions to the retreat center and I said that I did not. She then said perhaps there are directions in the vestibule. "Perfect", I thought. While I gathered my bass, she went back to the vestibule to look for directions. I then followed. As she was looking on one of the tables, I pulled out a gift bag and put it on the table in front of her. In the bag was a rose, a card and a small, hinged, porcelain figurine of Belle; the lead character in Beauty and the Beast. As she opened the hinged portion of the figurine, I quickly reached in the compartment and pulled out the engagement ring. I then took her hand and directed her back a few steps to the exact spot where we had met. I got on my knee and asked her to marry me. She, of course, said yes. I had truly surprised her. We then went up to the altar and knelt and prayed for our engagement and marriage.

In the opening scripture, Jesus said to His disciples, *"This cup is the new covenant in my blood…"* The words, *new covenant in my blood,* are the same words that a Jewish man of that time would use when proposing. He would say those words as he handed a cup of wine to the girl that he was proposing to. She didn't have to say a word. If she drank from the cup, she was saying yes. If she, on the other hand, did not drink, but handed the cup back… she was saying no. How surprised were the disciples who may have thought that Jesus was proposing to them as He handed them the cup. Since we are to be called the bride of Christ, I don't think it was a coincidence that Jesus used those words.

I know how special it felt when Kathy said yes to my proposal. She wanted to be my bride. How it must bless Jesus when you take communion and, in a sense, you are saying to Him, "Yes Lord… I want to be Your bride!"

RESCUING A ROBIN

Psalm 116:8 – 9 For You have rescued my soul from death, My eyes from tears, My feet from stumbling. I shall walk before the LORD In the land of the living.

My wife and I love sitting on our back porch and watch God's nature; clouds, stars, storms, birds. On one particular day we were doing just that. All of a sudden we heard a barrage of tweeting and screeching by a group of birds coming from between ours and the neighbors garage. We then caught sight of the neighbor's cat with something in its mouth. It was a bird. We both jumped up and went down the porch steps. The cat, in seeing us coming, dropped the bird and quickly ran and went over the fence between ours and the other neighbor's house. As I chased after the cat, Kathy went to the little bird that was laying in the grass and tweeting frantically. I then joined her and the bird got up on one leg and began hopping away from us. Its other leg was obviously injured. We knew we couldn't leave it like this or the cat would soon be back to claim its meal. It couldn't yet fly because, as we discovered later, it was a robin fledgling (a bird that has acquired its flight feathers, but hasn't yet flown).

I was able to scoop the little bird up and Kathy went to get a box. While in my hands, at first it protested, but then would calm down and close its eyes as if it were content and felt safe nestled there.

What a wonderful image of us and God. The enemy attacks us and, at times, even catches us and injures us. But God will jump up and come to our rescue and cause the enemy to release us and flee. God then scoops us up and cares for us. When we feel His hands holding us, a total tranquility and peace come over us and we find rest. He has rescued our soul from death, dried our tears and wants to help us recover from our injuries and pain. Instead of being swallowed up by the devour… we get to walk in the land of the living.

To continue with the story of the fledgling: I put it in the box and gave it some water and put some bread crumbs in with it (After further study, trying to feed it wasn't the best thing to do.). With it now beside me on the porch, as Kathy had to leave, I got on-line and learned the best thing to do with this little creature. According to what I read, mom and/or dad weren't too far off and they wanted to help their offspring to learn to fly. I needed to put him back out there for them to find and do what comes natural. However, I didn't want to expose the bird to any more danger from the cat. Although his leg seemed to be getting better, I didn't want to chance putting him in a nearby tree. Instead, there is a sizeable shed, across the alley from our house, with a low enough roof that I could reach up and place the bird there. There was also a vine growing up the side of it and into the rain gutter. I took the bird and placed it in the gutter amongst the vines and then went back to my porch. Soon I saw a few birds on the corner of the roof chirping at each other. A couple of them then flew off, but one hopped, on both legs, to the peak of the roof. Was that the fledgling? I took a walk back down to the shed and reached my hand up and into the gutter. The little bird was gone. As I turned around, I saw a little bird, several feet away, standing near the edge of the roof looking at me. I slowly walked toward it until I was only a couple of feet away. It was the fledgling. It didn't run from me, but instead calmly turned and hopped back up to the peak of the roof, on both legs, and then, although I couldn't see it clearly, I am pretty sure it flew off of the other side. It was as if it were thanking me and showing me that it was alright now.

We need to thank God constantly for the way he helps us and protects us. I, also, don't think that He minds if we happen to show Him that, because of what He has done for us, we are alright now.

(Picture 1) Fledgling in Paul's (my) hand
(Picture 2) The Fledgling in the box
(Picture 3) The shed that I placed the fledgling on.

SIGNS AND WONDERS

John 4:48 *So Jesus said to him, "Unless you people see signs and wonders, you simply will not believe."*

It amazes me that, otherwise, strong Christians get caught up in signs and wonders. It seems that they have to see someone performing some kind of a miracle or hear people speaking in tongues before they will believe that the Holy Spirit is at work in an individual or even a church. I often wonder if the words from John 4:48 will ever be self-applied at some point in their lives? I often question if they are like Thomas and need to see miracles to really believe? I also question; Is that really faith?

For the record: I do believe that "miracles by God" happen. I believe that some people are healed of even life threatening diseases; that God will protect some people in dangerous situations; that some people are given prophesies and words of knowledge; that some people are given the gift of tongues and others of interpretation of tongues. (SIDE NOTE: Tongues are not the only true evidence of the indwelling of the Holy Spirit. Not everyone who is saved and has the Holy Spirit speaks in tongues. Study 1 Corinthians 12:1 – 31 and 14:1 – 19). I also don't find any solid evidence in scripture that tells us that those miracles aren't for today as some people teach.

The question has to be, though, does everyone who claims a gift, really have that gift? I think that there are times the gifts are faked and that can be dangerous! I heard of a revival meeting at a church where the guest speaker began laying hands on people to heal them and also prophesy over them. He told one gentleman that he was healed of his depression and could stop taking his medication. The gentleman did. A few weeks later, that gentleman, otherwise mentally stable while on the medication, killed his wife and himself. Extreme example? Maybe… never-the-less, a true story.

So, how can one know what gift he/she has? Simple… you need do nothing. The Holy Spirit will do it through you. Example: You can't learn to speak in tongues! (I heard of a church that will teach you how to speak in tongues! How can you teach a gift that God decides if you should have it or not?!).

I can use myself as an example. As a baby Christian, the first church I went to was one that taught that speaking in tongues was the only true evidence of the indwelling of the Holy Spirit. I know that I loved the Lord and I had a strong faith in Jesus Christ (Ephesians 2:8 – 9), but I didn't speak in tongues. Did I have the Holy Spirit!? It bothered me so much that one evening when I was praying about it, I was in tears and cried out to the Lord, "I know that I love You. I feel as though I have Your Spirit within me yet I am being told that I need to speak in tongues! Show me the truth!" Almost as soon as I asked that of the Lord, it was as if every nerve in my body stood on edge and I uttered out a sentence (a short sentence at that) in an unknown tongue. I then felt in my spirit as thought the Lord was asking me if I was satisfied. I knew that I had His Spirit and I also knew that I was to never question it again! I've not said another word, via the Holy Spirit, in another tongue since. Yet I know that I have His Spirit living within me.

If you are going to seek signs and wonders, do as Paul says to do in 1 Corinthians 14:1 and seek the gift of prophesy. There are miraculous prophesies, but the simple definition of prophesy is to simply convey what God has shown you, to others. That means sharing His word, your testimonies, His love and how He brought you out of darkness and into His light. To share that miracle of salvation is the greatest sign and wonder of all.

SPEAK FROM YOUR HEART

Luke 6:45 *The good man out of the good treasure of his heart brings forth what is good; and the evil man out of the evil treasure brings forth what is evil; for his mouth speaks from that which fills his heart.*

Quit a long time ago, I use to be a serviceman for a small company. The company has since gone out of business, but during my twenty-plus years there, the company went through several personnel changes. There was one person that was hired that created some friction between himself and the service manager. As time went on, it got to be a very serious problem. It became so bad, that the service manager was always in a very angry mood and would take out his frustrations on all of us.

We finally complained to the upper management and their remedy was for all of us in service, to have a closed door meeting with the service manager. During the meeting, we told the serviceman and the manager that they needed to work this thing out. We told the serviceman to focus on his job and do what he was hired to do… as the rest of us were doing. We then told the service manager that he needed to have more patience with the tech and to also stop taking his frustrations out on the rest of us.

The thing that struck me, aside from the issues at hand, was the service manager's way of explaining his thoughts and feelings about everything that was going on. He constantly quoted lines from the sci-fi television/movie franchise; Star Trek. When I say that he quoted it: I would dare any Christian to be as precise and to the point with quoting Bible verses to state their case.

I'm not sure about either man's spiritual walk. Although I tried my best to evangelize while working at that facility, not everyone listened. As I think about that incident, though, I can only think of the opening verse above. Especially the last part of the verse: *for his mouth speaks from that which fills his heart.* (LUKE 6:45)

The service manager's attempt to make peace with us and his adversary was a plethora of quotes from a fictional show. The quotes were the philosophies of the writers and producers of that show. The results: peace didn't last long following that meeting and the serviceman eventually went too far and was fired. Once he was gone then there was peace again and the service manager was back to being his normal self.

As Christians, we have more solid words and a more meaningful show, written and produced by God, to use in problem solving. Had both of those men used Biblical principles to govern themselves, there would have been a much better ending.

If you name the name of Jesus, Than He should be what is in your heart and what you want to speak about. If you struggle with speaking about Jesus and His word more than worldly philosophies, than I would challenge you to do a self-examination.

SPIRIT OF PRIDE

Proverbs 16:18 *"Pride goes before destruction, And a haughty spirit before stumbling."*

Kathy and I enjoy going to Christian concerts. We love to enter in to worship while getting to see artists that have helped to encourage and inspire our walk with the Lord. These concerts bring people from different denominations and Christian backgrounds together. It is common to find Baptists, Methodist, Assembly of God, Presbyterians, Catholics and many others hearing, singing and responding to the songs being sung.

Quit a few years ago; within a one year span, we went to two Christian concerts where I was truly disappointed. Not in the artist or worship, but in the response by some people. Following the concert, I overheard some comments that went something like this:

* "It was great that our people were standing and worshipping. What was wrong with those other people!? We sure showed them how you're supposed to worship!'"

* "That concert was dead. No one stood up except our church. I'll never go and see that artist again."

As I stated; many churches are brought together in a concert. Different churches (and individuals) react differently when it comes to what happens during worship. Sitting may be a way that they respect the Lord in their worship. I will, at times, kneel when I really enter in. Just because someone doesn't stand, it's not up to us, but rather the Lord to judge what is in their heart.

When those comments were made, I thought of Jesus' parable in Luke 18:9-14. You know the story; The Pharisee and the Tax Collector who both went to the temple to pray. The Pharisee saying, 'look at me Lord how good I am'; The Tax Collector saying, 'forgive me Lord, a sinner'. I put my own twist to that scripture: *Two men went to hear an anointed worship leader. One was a member of a certain church and the other from a different church. The first person stood and was looking around to see who else was standing. He was also thinking this to himself: 'God, I thank You that I am not like other people from a different church who don't stand and worship you. I stand; I sing loudly so everyone knows that I'm worshipping.' But the other person was not looking around and he was singing so that only his Father in heaven could hear him. His heart was crying out. He was worshipping the Lord in spirit and in truth.*

For me, true worship is of the heart and not action. Example: My wife Kathy has respiratory and larynx problems. For that reason, she is to limit her speech and singing. Yet, I know that she loves worshipping the Lord and she does, even if it is in silence. Will someone, not knowing her heart, dare to judge her? *"Do not judge according to appearance, but judge with righteous judgment."* John 7:24

I once heard that pride is the root of most sin. I think that the most harmful pride is when we think that we are so righteous and pious before God over others. If they are in sin, then correct them and even rebuke them. However, if they are not sinning and you are just judging by their outward appearance and you feel that what you're doing is more pleasing to God than what they are doing… You need to repent and take Proverbs 16:18 to heart.

PS: Don't judge others while boasting of yourself. Instead, be humble and boast in the Lord so that <u>God</u> might commend you! 2 Corinthians 10:14 – 18

SPOILED BRATS

Proverbs 29:15 *The rod and reproof give wisdom, But a child who gets his own way brings shame to his mother.*

My wife and I, in our love of travel, went to California a several years back. Our main reason was to go to Disneyland. We've been to Walt Disney World in Florida, many times, but we wanted to experience the original of Mr. Disney's dreams. Now, even though we live in the jet age and travel is a lot easier than our grandparents had, it is still a major feat to travel almost all the way across the United States. For a middle income family, such as we are, the expense alone can be a spoiler. Then there is all of the time in planning and booking. There's the figuring out the ground transportation when you get there. You try and schedule everything so that you can get the most out of the experience knowing that it may be quite some time, if ever, before you return.

I am pleased to say that our trip was great. We got to see many sights in and around Los Angeles. Disneyland was everything that we imagined it would be.

A few weeks after we got home I heard a report about a child celebrating their birthday at Disneyland. I know that it probably is a common occurrence for children to celebrate their birthdays at an amusement park but, in this case, the parents, who were wealthy, bought out the park and had them close it to the public. I thought to myself, 'What if I had spent my hard earned money and travelled almost 3000 miles to go to Disneyland and they closed it so that this child could be entertained?'

It made me think of the opening scripture that tells us that a child that gets their own way brings shame to their mother. What the Bible is saying is that the parents are to be in control of their children. Too many parents are trying to be friends to their children and not parents. As a result, there is shame brought to the family, even if they don't realize it. The parents of the child I mentioned are probably clueless that others are thinking that their child is spoiled. That by doing that, it may have interfered with the plans and, especially, the investment of some that may only have the means to do something, such as visit Disneyland, once in a lifetime.

Train up a child in the way he should go, Even when he is old he will not depart from it. Proverbs 22:6 At some point, a child will leave father and mother and have to make their own decisions. Even with the best of love and parenting, there are still those children who will go astray. But, if you've done your job, as the scriptures instruct, then there is always hope. It's okay to be a friend to your child, but, be a parent first. They don't need to have Disneyland all to themselves. Don't let others say of them, behind your back, that they are spoiled brats. It isn't a good witness of being a Godly, Biblically obedient parent nor is it what God would have your children grow to be.

SUFFICIENT SCRAPS

Luke 16:19a; 20; 21a *Now there was a rich man.* **And a poor man named Lazarus was laid at his gate, covered with sores, and longing to be fed with the *crumbs* which were falling from the rich man's table.**

For as long as I can remember, I loved throwing old bread out in the yard and then watching the birds gather and feast. Recently, we had some old hot dog buns and I tossed them into the yard. In the process, there was one very small piece that got tossed. It wasn't heavy enough to travel very far and it landed on the sidewalk just off of our back porch. After I distributed the buns, I sat down on the porch and soon was entertained by many birds coming for lunch.

I especially watched the small piece that was on the sidewalk. It took a while, but finally one little bird flew down and began eating it. The parcel was so small that as the bird pecked at it, it was moving all over and crumbs were falling from it. Then another bird landed beside it and the first bird took the small piece of bread in its beak and flew off. I figured that the second bird would then make its way down to the bigger pieces of bread in the yard (all of which were surrounded by other birds pushing their way in to get a bite). To my surprise, it began picking up crumbs that were left from the small piece of bread. Once it had its fill, it flew off.

In this world, everyone seems to be out to get all that they can. Even in the Christian community, we find doctrines (that I don't mind going on record to call them false) that imply that we should have wealth and riches and health and everything that we desire. Then I look at the story that Jesus told in Luke 16:19 – 31 (which many feel is a true story and not a parable). I see that Lazarus' only desire was to have even the crumbs from the rich man's table. That would have been sufficient for him (Like with the little bird).

Another scripture I think of is 2 Corinthians 12:7. Paul tells of how God allowed a messenger from Satan to torment him with, what Paul calls, a thorn in the flesh. We're not privy to what that thorn was, but we know that Paul's desire was to be rid of it. We also know that God didn't remove it. Paul's response: *And God has said to me, "My grace is sufficient for you, for power is perfected in weakness." Most gladly, therefore, I will rather boast about my weaknesses, so that the power of Christ may dwell in me.* 2 Corinthians 12:9 God had His purpose for Paul's condition: so that Christ would be magnified… not Paul.

Both Lazarus, the beggar, and Paul experienced tormenting times in this world. Yet, both are now in heaven enjoying greater riches there then they could ever imagine here. God did pour out blessings on them for their faithfulness… spiritual and eternal blessings… not worldly.

As with the little bird; you may see others with big chunks of bread, but God may just want you to have what is sufficient. It may be to keep you humble and focused on Him and not being a part of a crowd that may be pushing and shoving for a worldly indulgence (believers and non-believers).

As for me in this life… I would rather have God's crumbs than a whole loaf of worldly bread. I know that there is a feast waiting for me in heaven. The life He's given me is sufficient… How about you?

THE COVER UP

Colossians 3:9 *Do not lie to one another, since you laid aside the old self with its evil practices...*

For those of you that can remember when home computers were a fairly new item to have in your house, they were quite expensive. I couldn't always afford to have a home computer. I did, however, get hooked on the internet and email. Quit a few years ago, when the old computer I had at home stopped working, I was able to keep up by using my computer at my work. As long as I did my job and my work got done, my superiors didn't have a problem with that.

There was, however, a weekend that I really wanted to use a computer at home. So, on Friday evening after work, I packed up the desk top computer and took it home with me. At the time, I was computer illiterate and in attempting to connect to the internet through a dial up system (remember those), I really messed something up.

Embarrassed and afraid of repercussions, I went in to work a little early on Monday morning and set my computer back up as if it had never left. Later that morning I summoned our IT and told him of the problems I was having connecting to the internet at the office. I figured he could have it fixed in no time. After asking me several questions that I either stretched the truth on or just out and out lied about, he took the computer and began working on it along with another computer literate co-worker. I could hear them in the adjoining office making statements like: "I think we were hacked!" "Someone must have tried to get in to our system." Eventually, the pressure got to me and I went in to that office and fessed up to what I did. The damage to the computer was to the extent that the IT had to format the hard drive and start all over again with new software.

Lies never end. Once you start to lie, you wind up having to lie more to support the previous lies that you told. In Paul's letter to the Colossians, he calls lying an evil practice that shouldn't be a part of our born again nature.

No doubt; I was wrong in taking an expensive piece of the companies equipment home with me. That wasn't sin though… it was just a stupid misjudgment. The sin was when I lied on Monday morning to try and cover up what I had done. Although I looked foolish by taking the computer home, the lying was worse. It gave pleasure to the enemy. How Satan loves it when Christians give in to sin… especially the sin that Jesus tells us that the devil is the father of (John 8:44).

But what I think is even worse than knowing that we are bringing pleasure to Satan; we're breaking the heart of our God because of our disobedience.

In Proverbs 6:17, we're told that, "a lying tongue," is an abomination to God. The Hebrew word for abomination is; *tow'ebah* – it's meaning = a disgusting thing equivalent to how God views idolatry. If you think about it, when we lie, it is mostly to make our favorite idol be free of guilt or to steer the blame away from that idol. The idol = ourselves. I know that you don't want to be that abomination before our Lord. Even in the worst situations, just be truthful. God knows we're going to do stupid things… children are like that. Don't allow it to become sin by trying to cover it up with lies.

THE FALL

Acts 12:11 *When Peter came to himself, he said, "Now I know for sure that the Lord has sent forth His angel and rescued me from the hand of Herod and from all that the Jewish people were expecting."*

On a particular January 12th, my day started out like any other day at the church. I had certain jobs that I wanted to accomplish. One of those jobs was to change the light bulb in the overhead projector that projects the words of our Sunday morning worship songs on a screen in the back of the sanctuary. I am not going to go into all of the details but, in the process of changing that bulb, I wound up falling, almost 20 feet, from that projector.

Miraculously, I came out of the fall with only a torn rotator cuff in my left shoulder. When I say miraculously, I don't use that term lightly or feel that is an exaggeration.

Several things that happened add up to more than just coincidence:

First; when the ladder fell, I was able to grab the mounting bracket of the projector and hold on to it instead of going down with the ladder and landing on it. Who knows what injuries that may have caused?

Second; when I did fall, I landed on my feet on the most flexible portion of the cushioned seat of the pew below. I was facing toward one end of the pew.

Third through fifth; Had I been a few inches to my right, I would have straddled the back of the pew. I would probably be a paraplegic or be dead and would not be writing this.

Had I landed a few inches to my left, I would have had one foot hit the pew and one miss thus causing me to hit the rear of the pew In front of the one I landed on. I probably would have broken some bones or had some other internal injuries.

Had I landed a few inches to my front or back on the pew, the bracing of the pew would have been more solid and it wouldn't have absorbed as much of the energy of the fall as it did. Where I did land on the pew, the wood under the padding actually cracked. (A co-worker and one of our deacons repaired it.)

I tell people, jokingly, that there was an angel there, hoping that his wings wouldn't fail him as he guided my path to the exact spot on the pew that I landed. Although I say it joking, I do feel that God had an angel watching over me that day. In Acts 12:11 (above), Peter says that he knew for sure that there was an angel sent from the Lord to protect him. I feel that there was one that day at the church to protect me also.

There are those who might ask, "Why did God allow it to happen in the first place?" I don't know the answer to that for certain. I do know what Jesus says in one of my favorite verses: *In the world you have tribulation, but take courage; I have overcome the world."* John 16:33b I know that I now have a deeper respect for the life that God has given me. I also know that he spared me for some reason and I need to be sensitive to what He wants me to do because of his mercy on that day.

Another reason may be found in Proverbs 19:25b, *But reprove one who has understanding and he will gain knowledge.* The word, 'Reprove', in the Hebrew is Yakach, which has a meaning of, 'to decide'; 'to correct'; 'to reason'. Perhaps God's reason was that He <u>wanted</u> me to learn from this experience and gain knowledge that I could share with others (IE: this tidbit). There are lessons for all of us to learn from everyday experiences.

Those experiences don't need to be as dramatic as my fall was. They can be everyday experiences. We just need to pay attention.

Whatever the reason, know that God does give charge to His angels, at times, to intercede for us. As a Christian, don't consider anything a coincidence. It may very well have been an angel's intervention and a lesson to learn.

WHEN MY FATHER PASSED AWAY

---

1 Thessalonians 4:13 *But we do not want you to be uninformed, brethren, about those who are asleep, so that you will not grieve as do the rest who have no hope.*

Although I was adopted by the person that I came to know as my father, he treated me like his own son and I loved him.

I was a senior in high school and it was the day after Thanksgiving. My father went in for surgery to remove gall stones. A nurse met us in the waiting room and said that the doctor wanted to meet with us. As we were following her through the hallway, the doctor walked toward us. He told us that he had opened my father up to remove the gall stones but, instead, found that he had advanced cancer in his liver and gall bladder. There wasn't much he could do so he just closed him back up. He then said that my father (at age 49) may have 2 months, if that, to live. I immediately collapsed to my knees. The doctor took us into a nearby examination room and broke an ammonia tablet under my nose.

I was not a Christian at that time. I went to church and was somewhat religious, but I had no true relationship with Jesus. Because of that, my understanding of death was that it was the ultimate defeat in life.

Now that I know Jesus and I also know that He is the ultimate defeat of death, I have a different perspective. That doesn't mean that I don't grieve when someone close to me dies… I will still miss them for the time that I have left here on earth. What it does mean is that I have hope of one day seeing them again in heaven.

Know also that it is not my place to judge if a person has made it into heaven or not. My father, as far as I know, didn't know the Lord. It would be easy for me to say that he is in Hell. Instead, I leave it at; "I don't know." I say that because two months and a week after receiving the prognosis from the doctor, my father was back in the hospital and we knew that he wouldn't be returning home. I wasn't with him for the whole duration of time that he was in there. The last time I saw him, hours before his death, the poisons in his blood due to his liver no longer filtering it, had gotten into his brain and he was totally unaware of anyone's presence. During my absence from him, while he was still in his right mind, did an evangelist visit him and lead him to Jesus? Now that I am a Christian, I can only hope so.

There are two lessons for us to take away from this:

First; We should not give up hope. Unless you know for a fact that someone died without repentance and coming to Jesus, there is still hope.

Second; We need to make sure that those that we care about, that are still with us, get to hear the true gospel.

We, as believers, should not be counted as, *"the rest who have no hope"* (1 Thessalonians 4:13).

WHO IS YOUR GOD?

James 4:10 *Humble yourselves in the presence of the Lord, and He will exalt you.*

We all tend to put others on a pedestal. It might be your husband, wife, a parent, a child or grandchild. We also tend to put things on a pedestal... ie: sports teams, politicians (I know... this may be a stretch) or even a church.

As an example: After I first got saved, I had a friend that lived nearby and we would ride to church together. He was very on fire for the Lord and was called upon at times to speak when the Pastor wasn't available. I remember one evening we were on our way to a weeknight service. Our conversation was about the preaching and teachings of the church. My friend made a comment that threw me. He said that if our Pastor would ever leave, he (my friend) would probably backslide.

My response was to question: "You would backslide? Then where is your faith!? Is your faith in the Pastor or is it in Jesus Christ? Who is your God?"

He agreed with me and said that he didn't know why he even made that statement. The bottom line is that he had raised the pastor up to such a high level that, even though he didn't really mean what he had said, the pastor had become somewhat of an idol to him. Unfortunately, the pastor did backslide and lost his ministry. My friend, I'm happy to say, remained strong in the faith.

The problem is that we are all human. We are going to stumble and even fall at times. We are definitely going to disappoint. We need to keep Jesus alone on a pedestal.

The other thing we NEED to do is to remain humble ourselves. We can also have a tendency to put ourselves on a pedestal. We like to think that we are always right or we are the best at what we do. Even if the facts support that you are that good, read the opening verse, James 4:10, above. Be humble and let God exalt you! Instead, when you boast, boast in the Lord (1 Corinthians 1:31).

As for me: I have a terrible time accepting compliments. I believe the profit Isaiah when he says in Isaiah 64:6 *For all of us have become like one who is unclean, And all our righteous deeds are like a filthy garment; And all of us wither like a leaf, And our iniquities, like the wind, take us away.* It's not that I don't do any good... but if it is truly good, than Jesus needs to get the praise. Because any righteousness that we have that is worthy of praise comes from Jesus. 2 Corinthians 5:21 *He made Him who knew no sin to be sin on our behalf, so that we might become the righteousness of God in Him* and Jeremiah 23:6 *In His days Judah will be saved, And Israel will dwell securely; And this is His name by which He will be called, 'The LORD our righteousness.'*

Finally, one of the worst abuses of putting others on pedestals, even amongst Christians, is worshipping celebrities and sports teams. I can't fault the unsaved... they need something to worship. I don't even have a problem with Christians liking a certain celebrity or rooting for a team. I do, however, have a problem when a celebrity or sports event takes precedence over things that would glorify God such as helping others in need. I've seen people miss church events because of a sporting event (professional, scholastic and amateur). I also know of churches that postpone or reschedule an event because of a "Big Game". I have to ask the question: "Who is their God?"

Now, ask yourself, and be honest... "Who or what is my God?" I pray that you will have the correct answer. That the same statement that was made about Abraham in Genesis 15:6 (*Then he* (Abraham) *believed in the LORD; and He reckoned it to him as righteousness*) can also be made of you.

WORKING IN A CHURCH

Psalm 84:10 (KJV) *For a day in thy courts is better than a thousand. I had rather be a doorkeeper in the house of my God, than to dwell in the tents of wickedness.*

At an airport on our way back home from a mission trip to El Salvador, one of my fellow travelers (and a member of our church) made a comment that was something to the effect: "You are so blessed being able to work at the church. I wish that I could work there."

I explained to him that his vision of my job was probably unrealistic and, knowing him, it wasn't what he would really like to do.

I know that people, that don't work in a church environment, probably visualize that we sit around all day reading our Bibles and praying when we're not encouraging others. Maybe there are some pastors and church staff out there that have that luxury… but that's not what I did. Having to deal with the maintenance of a sizable building that also houses a sizable daycare is work. I often tell people that I feel that I did a lot more one on one ministry when I worked a secular job. It's not that what I did wasn't ministry… but it's not the type of ministry that most would think that someone working in a church would do.

With that said, according to Psalm 84:10 (KJV) (above), I should not only be content, but I should feel special doing it. Or does it mean that? I have often heard that verse used in the context that it is about those that work or are at church. But if you read the whole Psalm, it clearly is talking about being in God's presence… not in a particular building or structure. Plus, remember, this was written when the Hebrew's felt that they had to go to the tabernacle to be close to God. Because of Jesus, we have Him, in the form of the Holy Spirit, living in us. We are always close to Him whether in a church or not.

Getting back to the Psalm; the word, "doorkeeper", is from the King James Bible. Other versions say that I would rather stand at the "threshold" of God's house. In either case, whether a doorkeeper or standing at the threshold, you are outside! Think about it… a doorkeeper at a fancy hotel stands outside. If you are at the threshold that means you haven't yet crossed it to go in. In short it is saying; I would rather be standing outside in the elements, but near to my God, rather than to be protected in the shelter of the wicked. Why? Psalm 84:11 (KJV) = *For the LORD God is a sun and shield*… HE brings you comfort and protects you even when you are exposed to the unpleasant elements of life!

It doesn't matter where you work; in a church or in an office or digging ditches, the rest of Psalm 84:11 and verse 12 (KJV) says if He is your God and you walk uprightly with Him, that He will give you grace and glory and He won't withhold good things from you.

Don't feel that just because someone works at a church that they are more blessed or special than you are. You have the same God, the same grace, the same Holy Spirit, the same opportunities for ministering. Draw close to Him right where you are. You will be blessed!

WRESTLING

Ephesians 6:12 (KJV) *For we wrestle not against flesh and blood, but against principalities, against powers, against the rulers of the darkness of this world, against spiritual wickedness in high places.*

Our oldest grandson has taken up wrestling in school. We went to a match recently to watch him. Have you ever watched a wrestling match (high school or college wrestling… not studio wrestling, on TV, which isn't the same)? There is a point in the match where one of the wrestlers gets down on his hands and knees and the other gets on his knees beside him. The top wrestler then puts his arm around the bottom wrestler and this is known as the referee's stance. The person on top, obviously, has the advantage here. The key for the bottom wrestler, and an opportunity for him to score points, is to escape and reverse the circumstances.

I started thinking about that picture from a spiritual point of view. Isn't that the way we are before we come to salvation. Satan has his arm wrapped tight around us and is waiting for the whistle to blow so that he can take us down. Our only counter move is to accept Jesus. Only with His salvation and redemption can we get out of Satan's hold and reverse the circumstances. Instead of him pinning us in Hell, we can score points by helping others to also get free by showing them the same move.

As in wrestling, the match isn't over once you escape. You need to keep wrestling until the time expires. Remember that Ephesians 6:12 (KJV) (above) is to the believer. Note that Paul even includes himself by saying,

"...*we wrestle*...". Jesus is going to get the overall victory, but if we just quit by not continuing to do our part for the kingdom, then we forfeit an opportunity for complete victory over Satan in our earthly lives. We need to continue to do our part in that spiritual match. To wrestle against those powers and principalities that attack us constantly.

Be aware though... there's nothing we can do in the flesh to overcome Satan's grip. It's only through the blood of Jesus and our testimony to others (Revelation 12:11) that he is ultimately defeated. The key to total victory is to keep doing the things that God has called us to do: pray, study the Bible, evangelize by sharing the gospel to the unsaved and use God's word to help encourage your fellow brothers and sisters in Christ.

Make no mistake about it, our enemy is strong. Jesus is stronger and it's because of Him that we're going to, one day, see Satan pinned and eliminated forever from wrestling anyone ever again. (Revelation 20:10)

WHY 'YOU CAN DO THAT'

---

1 Peter 4:10 *As each one has received a special gift, employ it in serving one another as good stewards of the manifold grace of God.*

While working at the church, the work load could get to be overbearing at times. There were enough everyday projects to keep us busy let alone special or unexpected tasks. In order to conquer some of the bigger projects, I, at one time, had started a ministry that I called, 'You Can Do That'. I had quite a few volunteers sign up to be a part of that ministry, each having their own gifts and talents to offer. Whenever a project would come up, I would have an announcement from the pulpit asking for help. I would also call the people on my list... especially those that I knew had a particular skill to help accomplish that particular job.

Part of the ministry was to get projects completed at the church. However, I also feel that part of it was to get others involved in the church. It's good to get involved in your church. In 1 Peter 4:10 (above) and also 11b, *whoever serves is to do so as one who is serving by the strength which God supplies; so that in all things God may be glorified through Jesus Christ, to whom belongs the glory and dominion forever and ever. Amen."* In short, by using the gifts and strength that God has already given to a person, especially through ministry, they are glorifying God.

Yes, it would be easy to say; "Why not hire someone to do the bigger projects at the church?" My reply: We are called to be good stewards in 1 Peter 4:10. If we have able bodied people, who God has equipped with special gifts and/or a servants heart, that can devote a couple of hours here or there to do the work instead of having to pay someone… that is being a good steward? It is also giving, those that help, an opportunity to be blessed for their efforts in serving the Kingdom. This can't be done with all projects. But, it's nice to do with those projects that it can be applied to.

In my example, the work being done is at the church that I attend. Perhaps there aren't that many needs within your church (I'm referring to the actual building). Then let there be service to others. You can help with projects at the homes of your members; help with projects with the poor or down trodden in your community (doing it in the name of the Lord); even going beyond and doing church sponsored mission's work where your gifts and talents can be utilized.

Our church has benefitted greatly from people from all walks of life that want to serve. Many serve through the various ministries that we have that fulfill the needs of our church. But they also serve individuals that are both members of our church and others not associated with our church. Their rewards are spiritual and eternal.

One last thought: The key here is not to do it for one's own gain or to please your pastor or others. More importantly, it's to do it so as to please the Lord out of your love for Him. "Whatever you do, do *your work heartily, as for the Lord rather than for men,*" Colossians 3:23

Use the gifts and talents that God has given you to bless your church and others. There are spiritual blessings awaiting those that do.

OTHER STORY TIDBITS

These stories aren't from personal experience. Rather they are stories that incorporate other story lines… some from movies, from TV, from cute little stories that I have heard. I have found that we can also learn from those. Even though the story we hear or the show that we are watching may not have any spiritual meaning to it, we can always learn a spiritual lesson from them.

AUNT BEE'S PICKLES

---

2 Timothy 3:10 (NLT) *But you, Timothy, certainly know what I teach, and how I live, and what my purpose in life is. You know my faith, my patience, my love, and my endurance.*

Kathy and I love watching reruns of the old Andy Griffith Show from the 1960s. There is one episode that comes to mind. Aunt Bee decided to make homemade pickles for the county fair contest. Her pickles, however, weren't good. In fact, they were terrible with the smell and taste of kerosene. She was determined to beat, her friend, Clara, who had won the blue ribbon several years in a row. Andy, Barney and Opie decided that they were going to help Aunt Bee win. They took all of her rancid pickles and ate them (for various reasons, it wasn't a good idea for them to dispose of the pickles in any other way). They replaced them with store bought pickles. It seemed like a good plan until Clara stopped in the courthouse to see Andy and showed him her scrap book with all of the blue ribbons she had won with her pickles. She explained how, since her husband had passed away, these ribbons gave her a reason to go on in life. To her, it was more than just winning a contest... it was her purpose in life. Andy and his cohorts then decided, for the sake of fairness and Clara, they needed to eat all of the store bought pickles and have Aunt Bee make a new batch of her kerosene pickles to enter in the fair. That's what they did and the result was that Clara won the contest.

In Paul's second letter to Timothy, chapter 3, he prophesy's about the wickedness of people as the last days approach. But then, in 2 Timothy

3:10 (NLT) (above), he says to Timothy that you know my purpose in life. We know that Paul's purpose was to take the gospel to the gentiles... those of us that aren't blood born Jew's. He also tells of his traits and sacrifices in doing so (2 Timothy 3:11 (NLT)).

Paul knew his purpose and calling. Do you? Have you asked the Lord to show you what He wants you to accomplish here on earth? Have you even asked what He would like you to do the rest of today... or tomorrow... or your life? It's important for us, who call ourselves Christians, to have that purpose. We're not to be on-lookers. We're to have an active role.

However, understand that being active in your walk will come with a price. Paul says this: *"Yes, and everyone who wants to live a godly life in Christ Jesus will suffer persecution."* So, as you say yes to God, be prepared for those persecutions to come. (2 Timothy 3:12)

For a 1960's sitcom, simply making a prize winning pickle is an OK purpose in life. But, in the real world of Christianity, we must go way deeper and become way more involved. Paul tells us that we are to do the work of an evangelist (2 Timothy 4:5). James says that if we say we have faith (in Christ and the gospel He gave us) but don't show it with works... That faith is dead (James 2:26). In Paul's letter to the Ephesians, he says that Christ gave leadership to some (perhaps even you) *for the equipping of the saints for the work of service, to the building up of the body of Christ.* (4:11 – 12)

Clara worked hard to make her pickles prize winners. How hard should we work to the building up of the body of Christ? Seek the Lord for His purpose in your life towards building up the body of Christ. Then start making your "prize pickles".

DAMAGING GOSSIP

Proverbs 20:19 - *He who goes about as a slanderer reveals secrets, Therefore do not associate with a gossip.*

Let's face facts; we ALL like a juicy story. Don't deny it, just accept it as fact. But, according to the proverb above, we should avoid such conversation let alone repeat it ourselves. We are not representing Jesus very well when we, as His representatives (you know... Christians) find satisfaction in spreading rumors (Gossip) - simply because it sounds good.

Although rumors and gossip are wrong, it seems especially bad when you do it to try and prove or disprove scripture so as to draw non-believers in. Here is an example:

I once heard it said that NASA proved that there is a day missing in history and they traced it back to the Bible: where the sun stood still for Joshua (Joshua 10:13) and where it went backwards for Hezekiah (2 Kings 20:8-11). In researching this, I found that this story of science proving a missing day came out long before NASA even existed. It was just modernized at some point. It's simply not true. It sounds wonderful, but it's a lie and we, as Christians, are spreading it. (Remember who the 'father of lies' is). Christianity strongly relies on FAITH. We don't need science to tell us what we should know by faith.

Another way Christians give Christianity a bad name, through spreading gossip, is by condemning people, places or things that do something that we disagree with, without really investigating if it's the truth.

One example: Apparently, there is a weekend every year where the gay and lesbian community gets together at Walt Disney World in Florida. The rumor is that WDW promotes and supports those days. That is not true. The gay community does their own promotions and purchase tickets from WDW the same as any other group would. Walt Disney World can't deny them the right to purchase the tickets. Yet, I know Christians that won't go to WDW because they falsely believe that WDW supports those days. They also actively spread that rumor as truth. Understand, I don't have stock in Disney, but if you're going to talk about them, or anyone else, then get the facts straight. Don't gossip or spread a rumor! *"But I tell you that every careless word that people speak, they shall give an accounting for it in the Day of Judgment. For by your words you will be justified, and by your words you will be condemned."* Matthew 12:36 – 37

With today's technology, it is very easy for someone to verify a story. It would be simple for a non-Christian to check out the above stories. But more so, I think we should use that technology to our advantage and make sure we have all of the facts straight so that we are being truthful in our witnessing.

If you weren't a Christian, would either of the above stories help to draw you to Christianity? I think more so, they would cause you to scratch your head and ask; 'Why should I become a Christian when they need to spread rumors and lies to try and add to their numbers?' Don't allow yourself to be deceived. Investigate the truth and don't be a spreader of gossip or rumors. Concentrate more on spreading the Gospel instead of gossip and allow God's truth to speak for itself.

DERISHAH

---

2 Timothy 2:15 (KJV) *Study to shew thyself approved unto God, a workman that needs not to be ashamed, rightly dividing the word of truth*

My wife and I have been to Israel on a few teaching tours. We have acquired teachings that we had never heard before.

Some of the teachings are complex and dwell deep in the history and culture of the people referenced in the scriptures. By knowing that, we can better understand why certain things were written and a deeper meaning as a result of that knowledge.

There are also some simpler teachings that we brought back. A 'derishah' is such a teaching. The Hebrew word 'derishah' simply means to look deeper. In particular, the rabbi's will look deeper at complex, troublesome scriptures so that they can make them understandable to the people.

When we share with others, we use the word, derishah, when we are conveying something the Lord has shown us about a particular scripture or Bible story. It is usually not a long explanation, but just conveys the findings of the person sharing that particular teaching. This involves, on the part of the sharer, a deeper study by them to fully understand what they have been taught and what they are to teach about that scripture. Plus, it should be meaningful to them and pertinent to those that they are sharing it with.

Paul, in his second letter to Timothy (2:15 KJV), tells us that we should study God's word and not just read over it. He goes as far as to say that we need to do so to show ourselves approved unto God. The Greek word used for study in that verse is, 'Spoudazo'. It also means to be diligent, which is used in other versions of the Bible, such as the NASB. Diligent in what? If you read the rest of 2 Timothy 2:15, it is saying to be diligent in rightly dividing the word of truth – the scriptures (Bible).

I took a homiletics class through my church. As part of the class, we were to, twice, share a 10 minute message before the pastor and the other students. In one of my messages, I grossly misrepresented a scripture to try and prove my point. My pastor knew the scripture well and knew that it didn't pertain to what I was talking about. He called me out on it. He explained that if I was giving that message in a real sense and those listening would study that scripture and find out that I had misrepresented it, it could nullify my whole message.

It's important to always convey God's word in truth. To misquote or misrepresent a scripture or story in the Bible is to lie. Besides, if you are on track with what you want to convey, the Word will support it without having to use wrong scriptures.

Share God's word; but as Paul says in 2 Timothy 4:2, *be ready...!* Don't just read the scriptures to say that you read them. Study them so that you will be equipped (2 Timothy 3:16 – 17) and rightly divide the God's word.

DON'T STEP ON THE DUCKS

---

1 John 1:8 *If we say that we have no sin, we are deceiving ourselves and the truth is not in us.*

I want to share this cute little fictional story that I heard some years ago:

> Jack died and went to heaven. As he was entering the gates, he noticed that there were ducks walking all over the place. "What's with the ducks?" he asked the angel at the gate. Just then, not far from them, a man stepped on a duck. Almost immediately, a woman, that obviously was not concerned about how she looked, appeared and was hand cuffed to the one that stepped on the duck. Jack understood that if you step on a duck, you'll be shackled to someone for eternity that you may not enjoy being with.

> Approximately 10 years later, Jack was minding his own business, and the ducks, when all of a sudden he found himself whisked away to another part of heaven. He was immediately hand cuffed to the most beautiful girl he had ever seen. "WOW," Jack exclaimed with glee! "What did I do to deserve this!?"

> "I don't know what you did," the girl said sobbing, "but I stepped on a duck."

Very demoralizing for Jack, I'm sure. Of course this is fictional... but there's an important lesson that can be learned from it. Most of us view ourselves through rose colored glasses. Even if we know that we may not be the handsomest or the smartest, we still are confident about some aspect of our life. It may even be our confidence in our spiritual walk. In the story above, Jack walked the straight and narrow and didn't step on any ducks. In the end, though, he discovered that he had his flaws.

As true believing Christians, our flaws are often our un-repented sins that we feel are okay. We brush them off with excuses. Examples: It was just a little white lie (a lie is a lie – 9th commandment – Exodus 20:16); Taking something small home, from my employer, without asking for it isn't going to hurt anything. (do not steal – 8th commandment – Exodus 20:15). That's just a couple of examples... I'm sure if you thought about it, you could come up with more. But, also, there is the sin of omission. Knowing that you should be doing something for God, yet you're not doing it. Examples: not taking an active part in your church or serving in some capacity (James 2:20 – 26); not befriending someone because they are different from you even though you feel that the Lord wants you to disciple them (Jesus' command – Mark 28:19); and so on. Side Note: Let me encourage you to also read 1 John 1:9 – 10.

In the story above, Jack was clueless and thought he was OK. Had he been more aware of his flaws and worked on correcting them (In his case, his appearance), he may not have been the one to disappoint the girl.

Take a closer look at your life and lifestyle. If after a thorough examination, you still say that you have no sin... go back to the beginning of this tidbit and read the scripture and then examine yourself again. Then, most importantly, if you're serious about pleasing the Lord, do something about it. Don't be like Jack... It won't be the girl you'll disappoint... It may be your Father in heaven.

MAKING PICKLES

Matthew 3:11 *As for me, I baptize you with water for repentance, but He who is coming after me is mightier than I, and I am not fit to remove His sandals; He will baptize you with the Holy Spirit and fire.* **(These are the words of John the Baptist)**

I was water baptized (the baptism of John) 4 times in my life:

The first time; According to my mother, because I was born pre-maturely and was so small, I was baptized (Sprinkled as a baby) and given the last rights by the church that my mom belonged to.

The second time; I gave my life to Jesus when my first marriage ended. It was my mother-in-law that I turned to and prayed with to receive Christ. Her church believed that water baptism was essential for salvation (I now know better) and I let her baptize me in her bath tub.

The third time; was with the first church that I went to after becoming a Christian. It was in a swimming pool of one of the congregation members.

The fourth time; When I went to Israel the first time, on a teaching tour, one of the stops was at the Jordan river. We learned of the Baptism of John and that even Jesus allowed John to baptize Him. We then did our own baptisms in the Jordan River.

The Greek word used most commonly in the New Testament is baptizo which is derived from a primary word, bapto. Apparently, even the ancient Greeks struggled with the exact meaning of the two words. Around 200 BC, a Greek named Nicander came up with a way to best end the confusion. He explained that when you make a pickle from a cucumber, you dip (bapto) the vegetable in boiling water. You now have a hot and soggy cucumber. Then, you would immerse (baptizo) the cucumber in a vinegar solution and it would chemically change and become a pickle.

The primary word, bapto was used most commonly, in the scriptures, where it mentions dipping or to dip. Example: John 13:26 - *Jesus then answered, "That is the one for whom I shall dip* (bapto) *the morsel and give it to him." So when He had dipped* (bapto) *the morsel, He took and gave it to Judas, the son of Simon Iscariot.*

Here's an example of Baptizo: Mark 10:39 *They said to Him, "We are able." And Jesus said to them, "The cup that I drink you shall drink; and you shall be baptized* (baptizo) *with the baptism* (baptisma) *with which I am baptized (baptizo)."* Notice that the word, 'baptism', uses a different Greek word. Baptisma is derived from baptizo. It's meaning is that of being cleansed or pardoned of ones sins through the acceptance of Christ. What Mark 10:39 is saying to the disciples and to us, is that we are to be immersed in Jesus' spiritual cleansing and forgiveness and as a result, be changed.

That's when we become pickles. If you're immersed in water without the change, than you are just a soggy cucumber (bapto). If you haven't yet done so, you can become a pickle today. Repent of your sinful life (Romans 3:23) and give yourself over to Christ. Allow Him to be the true Lord of your life. Allow Him to change you (baptisma). After all, He's a master pickle maker.

WITHOUT THEIR
POLITICAL ADVICE?

Mark 7:21 – 22 *For from within, out of the heart of men, proceed the evil thoughts, fornications, thefts, murders, adulteries, deeds of coveting and wickedness, as well as deceit, sensuality, envy, slander, pride and foolishness.*

"Get Smart" was a 1960's TV sitcom that parodied the popular spy genre of that time. As with a lot of the old television shows from the 50's, 60's and 70's, Hollywood likes to bring them back, with a remake, on the big screen. They did it with "Star Trek", "The Beverly Hillbillies", "The Wild, Wild West", "The Man From U.N.C.L.E.", "Mission Impossible" and others.

In 2008, there was a remake of "Get Smart". A quick plot synopsis: The bad guys have a nuclear bomb and want the United States to pay them an enormous sum of money to keep from exploding it and killing a lot of people. When the U.S. decides not to take them serious and not pay it, the chief bad guy chooses Hollywood as his target to explode the bomb. The timing to set it off is when the President of the United States is in Hollywood attending a concert. Of course, Maxwell Smart and Control thwart the bad guy's plans in the nick of time.

There is one line in the movie that is my favorite… probably because it holds so much truth. When the bad guys assistant comments about all of the Hollywood actors that will be killed, the chief bad guy answers satirically; "What will we do without their razor-sharp political advice?" It has become pretty common for some actors, singers and athletes to use their platform of fame to promote their political views. And, if you disagree with them, then you're the radical. However, there are a lot of people who are so taken by their favorite artists, that they will agree with their opinions regardless of its validity.

Mark 7:21 – 22 (above), besides being a truth for that time, it is also a prophecy by Jesus for all times. For my purpose here, I want to reflect on the pride and foolishness. Most people will gladly give their opinions on any subject matter that you can think of. Opinions are OK. The problem is when you feel as though your opinion is the only correct one without really studying the validity of other opinions. More important than having and sharing your opinion is to also listen (and learn).

As Christians, I've found that we also have a tendency to share our opinions with God. An example would be: "Lord, if you would allow me to be rich, think of how much more I could do for the Kingdom!" That's not sin or even a bad thing. God wants to hear from us. What's important is to then take time to listen. Ask God what His thoughts are. He may not want you rich so that He can use you for His glory where you are.

If you're reading this, you probably aren't taken in by a famous person's view (This can also include famous Christian radio or television personalities or authors). Know that God isn't taken in by our views. He only wants to do what's right for us and for those that we encounter. Let's humble ourselves before the Lord and not sound foolish. Yes, let your petitions be made known to God. But then accept what His decision is concerning those petitions not being so prideful that you think that you know more. Our God is a God of great wisdom His opinion is the only one that is truly correct – Always!

SOME BIBLE
TEACHING TIDBITS

Here are some basic Bible teachings that God gave me. You will find other Bible teachings that I've placed in other chapters because I felt that they were appropriate for the particular topics of those chapters. Those that are in this chapter are, what I call, stand alone. I may have been able to assign them to other chapters, but didn't feel that, even though they may touch on that chapters subject, that isn't the main strength of these tidbits.

DEMONIAC TO DISCIPLE

Mark 16:15 *And He said to them, "Go into all the world and preach the gospel to all creation."*

"They (Jesus and His disciples) came to the other side of the sea, into the country of the Gerasenes." (Mark 5:1). The Gerasenes were located either in or on the fringe of an area, known in Jesus' time, as the Decapolis (meaning Ten Cities). We know that the Decapolis was a very Pagan area. They worshipped Roman and Greek gods as well as other Pagan gods.

In - *"When He (Jesus) got out of the boat, immediately a man from the tombs with an unclean spirit met Him,"* (Mark 5:2). There are 3 things that we know about this man: 1) He was possessed by many demons; 2) He was naked (as told in other gospels); 3) He was probably battered, bruised and bloodied because he would gash himself with stones.

As you continue to read Mark 5:2 through verse 17 you find Jesus confronting the demons that possess this poor soul and He casts them out into a herd of pigs (now think of where you are… Israel – why are they raising pigs?! Very non-kosher! The answer – they were raising them for sacrifice in their idol worship… more proof of their idolatry.) The herd of pigs than ran into the sea and drowned. Jesus became very unpopular with the pig farmers and was asked to leave… which He did. But first, He commanded the man that He had cleansed of the unclean spirits: *"Go home to your people and report to them what great things the Lord has done for you, and how He had mercy on you."* (Mark 5:19)

Now, let's go forward just a couple of chapters to Mark 7:31. We find Jesus traveling: *"Again He went out from the region of Tyre, and came through Sidon to the Sea of Galilee, within the region of **Decapolis**."* Jesus is back where He had encountered the demoniac. Mark 7:32 tells how a man was then brought to Jesus that was deaf and couldn't speak well. In Mark 7:33, it says: *"Jesus took him aside from the __crowd__........."* CROWD!? What Crowd? Remember, Jesus' first visit to this region had Him being greeted by <u>one</u> demon possessed man and a herd of pigs. What happened?!

I think the answer can be found back in chapter 5, after Jesus told the, now healed, man to go and tell his people what great thing the Lord had done for him. - *"And he (the demoniac) went away and began to <u>PROCLAIM IN DECAPOLIS</u> what great things Jesus had done for him; and **everyone was amazed**."* (Mark 5:20) He did as Jesus had told him to do and began spreading the word. If we read further to Mark 8:1 - 9, we find that that's probably geographically close to where Jesus fed the 4000 (that's just men and doesn't include women and children). Could one man have done this? I say yes!

Perhaps, at one time, you were that demoniac. Oh, you may not have been possessed by demons, but, you were of the world. Now, Jesus has spiritually healed you. How have you affected your part of the world because of that miracle? (NOTE: It's no less a miracle than what Jesus did for the demoniac). If Jesus would return to your territory, in the flesh, today, would a 'Crowd' gather because of your witness? If not... why not? If you believe God's word, then you must believe Mark 16:15 (the opening verse above). According to that scripture, it's our duty to share the Gospel.

The good news is that it is not too late to start. I realize it may be difficult at times, but think of the world that the demon possessed man had to go to. Yet, he got the job done. It's your turn to get the job done in your Decapolis.

DISCIPLING THE EVANGELIST

Acts 18:24 – 26 *Now a Jew named Apollos, an Alexandrian by birth, an eloquent man, came to Ephesus; and he was mighty in the Scriptures. This man had been instructed in the way of the Lord; and being fervent in spirit, he was speaking and teaching accurately the things concerning Jesus, being acquainted only with the baptism of John; and he began to speak out boldly in the synagogue. But when Priscilla and Aquila heard him, they took him aside and explained to him the way of God more accurately.*

From the scriptures above, what do we know about Apollos?

1) He was Jewish – But was born in the Alexandria region of Egypt.
2) He was, 'Eloquent' – Greek = logios = learned in arts; history; literature – also well-spoken and probably considered wise.
3) He was mighty in the scriptures. Part of that's due to his eloquence but a greater part of that would be because of his Jewish upbringing. This would be a tribute to his parents. When living in Egypt, it would have been extremely difficult to practice their Jewish faith. They would have not been treated well yet they still kept their faith and taught Apollos.
4) He was instructed in the way of the Lord – speaking and teaching accurately the things concerning Jesus (This tells us that someone shared Jesus with him!).
5) He was fervent in spirit. In short, he was excited to share <u>what he knew</u> of the gospel.

6) He was bold in the synagogue – he had to be bold to speak of Jesus because most Jews were opposed to the Christian teachings.

7) He was only acquainted with the baptism of John. He knew of the sign of the times and that Jesus was the Messiah. He also knew that John had prepared the way and repentance was necessary, but he didn't fully understand the meaning of Jesus' death and resurrection.

Aquila and Pricilla pulled Apollos aside and explained the <u>whole Gospel</u> to him. He accepted their corrections and teaching.

If Aquila and Pricilla became believers when Paul came to stay with them in Corinth… they, themselves, were still baby Christians of only a couple of years! Still, they knew more than Apollos so they were able to disciple him. As a result, we read in Acts 18:27 – 28, that Apollos leaves Ephesus and goes to Corinth and convinces many Jews that Jesus was the Christ.

Perhaps you feel unequipped to be sharing or teaching others. The question you should ask yourself, though, "Do I know more than they do?" If your answer is, "Yes", than share, teach, exhort, etc. We're called to evangelize (2 Timothy 4:5) and to make disciples (Matthew 28:19) and the way to do that is to share the true, COMPLETE gospel. Share what you know. Teach Sunday school. Hold a Bible study.

It's also important that you continue to grow yourself. That comes with STUDYING God's word (2 Timothy 2:15 & 3:16 – 17). Also, be teachable yourself (Thinking you know everything is the first sign that you really don't). The more you're willing to learn, as Apollos was, the more equipped you are to teach the truth. Finally, because someone was willing to teach Apollos, in 1 Corinthians 3:6, Paul credits him equally with himself - *I planted, Apollos watered, but God was causing the growth.* (NOTE: The key to this verse… Do God's work, but know that the end result should always point toward God… not self!)

DISPOSABLE SOCIETY

Malachi 2:16 - "*For I hate divorce,*" says the LORD, the God of Israel, "*and him who covers his garment with wrong,*" says the LORD of hosts. "*So take heed to your spirit, that you do not deal treacherously.*"

Have you ever seen multiple dumpsters behind a restaurant knowing that there is probably a large portion of food scraps in them? Or, when opening the packaging of a new item, had to go through layers of paper and plastic to get to the merchandise? All of that packaging will eventually be thrown out. We are living in a disposable society.

Unfortunately, it doesn't stop with just products. It also happens in life:

> ➢ Disposable babies. From 1973 (when abortions were legalized) thru 2011, 53 million abortions were performed in the United States; mostly for convenience sake… not health issues. Now there is a leaning toward partial birth abortions - Defined by Google: A late term abortion of a fetus that is KILLED before being completely removed from the mother. (Read Proverbs 6:16 – 17)
>
> ➢ Disposable elderly and/or sick or disabled: Euthanasia (the act of assisted suicide) is now legal in some European countries. Hitler practiced this during his reign in Germany with mentally and

physically handicapped people. (Again read: Proverbs 6:16 – 17 & Leviticus 19:32)

➤ Disposable marriages: 50% of first time marriages and 60% of second time marriages will end in divorce. The Christian community isn't exempt from divorce. Harvard trained researcher, Shaunti Feldhahn did an eight year study and found that 15 to 20% of all Christian marriages (first time, second time, third time and so on) will end in divorce. It's not God's plan for marriage to be disposable. (See the opening verse, Malachi 2:16, above).

I'd like to key on the disposable marriage… Causes:

1) Discontentment: As children, we are constantly told in fairy tales that we get married and live, "Happily Ever After". There may be a few marriages like that, but most have rocky areas in them. A lot of the rocky areas can be worked out within the marriage, but in more severe cases, a counselor needs to be involved.

2) Abuse: Perhaps one area that if it can't be remedied (that the person doing the abusing is willing to get help and quit), than for the safety of the spouse, a permanent separation/divorce may be in order.

3) Adultery: The grass seems to always look greener on the other side. I refer back to the statistic above, under disposable marriages; 60% of second timers end in divorce… I don't have the statistics, but I feel I can safely say that some of those second marriages, ending in divorce, are a result of one or both partners betraying their former spouses to have that relationship.

Solution: Read God's word and learn <u>His will and plan</u> for your marriage. The Bible has a lot of instructions about marriage. It's a matter of being obedient to those instructions.

This topic is dear to my heart because I've been there. My first marriage ended and my ex-wife remarried. Since then, my ex-wife and her, now husband, have become Christians. I give them credit because they did what Christians should do. They both came to me, on separate occasions, and asked for forgiveness. I know that when they asked Christ for forgiveness, He gave it to them and I did likewise (actually even before they asked for it)). Even though we weren't Christians when we married, it was not God's plan for our marriage to be disposed of. Even though it wasn't His desire for our divorce, He still was willing to extend His grace and mercy to all 3 of us (yes, I include myself in the mix as I had an opportunity to accept Jesus and then lead my family to Him before the marriage ended. Because I failed in that, I am not blameless). We have sought His forgiveness and He has given it.

Don't be a part of a disposable society and maybe have to experience God's consequences. Do what's necessary to make your marriage work! After all, you are to be the Bride of Christ. Will you divorce Him also?

A few scriptures to look up: Ecclesiastes 4:12 (3rd strand = Jesus); 1 Corinthians 7:10 – 16, 27, 33, 39; Genesis 2:23 - 25

DOCTRINAL DIFFERENCES

---

2 Timothy 4:3 *For the time will come when they will not endure sound doctrine; but wanting to have their ears tickled, they will accumulate for themselves teachers in accordance to their own desires*

If you've been a Christian for any length of time, I'm sure that you have had conversations with other Christians concerning doctrines. Sometimes you're in agreement and sometimes you're not. So, how do we determine what doctrines are correct and which ones aren't?

As Christians, there are certain doctrines that we must all agree with: There is only one God; the God of Abraham, Isaac and Jacob (Deuteronomy 6:4). That God exists in three persons; the Father, the Son and the Holy Spirit (John 14:9 – 20). The deity of Christ (John 1:1 & 14). He is the Messiah (Matthew 1:16). That He died for our sins (1 Corinthians 15:3), He rose again to conquer death (Romans 6:8 – 9) and He ascended into Heaven to prepare a place for us (Acts 1:9 & John 14:2 – 3 NASB). That we are saved by Grace through Faith (Faith in Jesus Christ and His words) and not by works (Ephesians 2:8).

But what about other doctrines? Doctrines such as the rapture (Pre, mid or post tribulation); Once saved, always saved; baptism (Sprinkled or dunked; babies or adult). I am not writing this tidbit to debate doctrine. I don't have a problem debating what I believe. However, even with that, I don't feel it should be argumentative. Especially, if the doctrine in question, has nothing to do with someone's faith or walk with the Lord.

As for those doctrines (those I've listed and others that I'm sure you can think of), I feel that the Lord showed me early in my Christian walk how to deal with them. I questioned some of the doctrines that were being taught at the first church I attended after coming to salvation. As I prayed about them, I felt the Lord tell me in my spirit, "If it's not crystal clear in the scriptures, than it's not something to get hung up on." The Rapture is an example and one that I struggled with. If you read Daniel and Revelation, there are points that support all three theories. I felt the Lord tell me, "It's not important as to when it will happen as long as you're ready" (Matthew 25:1 – 13).

If a brother or sister truly loves the Lord, then don't quibble over minor doctrinal differences. Instead, join forces to come against the real enemy. Combine to share sound doctrine and the love of Jesus. But, we also know that Jesus didn't tickle any ears. Be firm in sharing what it takes to follow the Lord… commitment and perseverance.

Most of all, Jesus summed up His whole doctrine in Matthew 22:37 – 40: *And He said to him, "'YOU SHALL LOVE THE LORD YOUR GOD WITH ALL YOUR HEART, AND WITH ALL YOUR SOUL, AND WITH ALL YOUR MIND.' "This is the great and foremost commandment. "The second is like it, 'YOU SHALL LOVE YOUR NEIGHBOR AS YOURSELF.' "On these two commandments depend the whole Law and the Prophets."* This is the foundational, and most important, doctrine of Christianity… To love God and to love others. That's Jesus' yoke and a solid doctrine that we should all be in agreement with.

EYES OPEN; EYES SHUT

---

2 Kings 6:8 – 23 – If you have a Bible handy, please read these verses (NOTE: It doesn't have to be the NASB. Feel free to read it in what ever version you have handy). If not, here's what's happening:

Aram was warring against Israel. The King of Aram was ticked because the King of Israel seemed to know his every move. One of the King of Aram's servants had to tell him that Elisha has been telling the King of Israel what he, the King of Aram, talks about in his bedroom. The servant also told him where Elisha could be found.

The King of Aram then sent a great army, by night, to capture Elisha. In the morning the servant of Elisha saw the army and was afraid. Then Elisha prayed and the Lord opened the servant's eyes to be able to see the Angelic army which was greater than the Aramean army.

When the Aramean army came to confront Elisha, he prayed that the Aramean army would be blinded. I feel that this was a spiritual blindness, not a natural one. Why? The Aramean's wouldn't be interested in finding Elisha anymore if they suddenly lost their physical sight. They would be stumbling around and would, undoubtedly, be very afraid. I know if I were suddenly struck blind, I would be afraid. (The Apostle Paul wouldn't eat for three days while he was blind (Acts 9:9)). Because of that spiritual blindness, they couldn't recognize Elisha (a Man of God) and they wound up following him into a trap at Samaria where the King of Israel was. Then their eyes were opened and they saw their predicament.

The King of Israel asked Elisha, *"Shall I kill them? Shall I kill them?"* (2 Kings 6:22) (Note: whenever you see something in a verse more than once, it may not have really been said twice. It was a way for the author to emphasize that the king, in this instance, really wanted to kill them.) Elisha didn't allow the King of Israel to kill them but instead to bless them and send them on their way. In 2 Kings 6:23, it says that the, *"marauding bands of Aramean's did not come again into the land of Israel."* In 2 Kings 6:24 we find the King of Aram surrounding Samaria, but, we know that at least that marauding band of Aramean's weren't accompanying him.

Using this story, I want to make a comparison of spiritual eyes open vs. spiritual eyes shut:

1) With eyes open; Elisha saw the enemies activities and warned the King of Israel.
   With eyes shut; The King of Aram didn't even know who his enemy was until one of his servants told him.
   The point: Desire that God opens your eyes to what the enemy is trying to do in your life! Don't wait for others to tell you… they could be wrong.

2) With eyes open; Elisha was peacefully asleep at home (I know that sounds like an oxymoron: his eyes open yet asleep. Elisha was able to rest because he knew God had his back
   With eyes shut; The Aramean's were, literally, stumbling in the dark! More than likely, as they approached the city, they probably doused their torches so as to not be detected and give a warning to Elisha.
   The point: Don't try to accomplish goals in worldly darkness. Instead, rest in the Lord and let God lead you in His light.

3) With eyes open; Elisha's servant saw victory!
   With eyes shut (Just prior to that) his servant saw calamity and was fearful!
   The point: Don't give up hope and don't fear… wait for God to open your eyes to <u>His plan</u> in your life. (*'For I know the plans that I have for*

you,' declares the LORD, 'plans for welfare and not for calamity to give you a future and a hope.' Jeremiah 29:11)

4) With eyes open; Elisha was able to lead the blind and even protect them from the angelic army surrounding them.
With eyes shut; The Aramean's didn't even recognize the man of God or that they were being lead into a trap.

The point: Pray that your spiritual eyes would always be open. When they are, be willing to lead the spiritual blind – bless them – it could lead to their salvation and their eyes also being opened!

HE'S NOT HIDING

Deuteronomy 4:29 - *But from there you will seek the Lord your God, and you will find Him if you search for Him with all your heart and all your soul.*

As you read Deuteronomy 4 beginning in verse 1, you find that Moses is recounting the Exodus, instructing and also prophesying about Israel's future with idolatry. As a result, they will be scattered! But, in Deuteronomy 4:29, he tells of their redemption and how they will once again find the Lord. However, he also tells of the conditions. (As you read any and all of God's promises, you find that there are always conditions.) They need to seek the Lord... but not just lightly; they need to search with <u>all</u> their heart and soul.

Even as believers, we also need to daily seek the Lord. And not just half-hearted! So, how do we do that? Below, I have listed what I call; 'Adverbial ways to seek the Lord' (You remember from school the definition of what an adverb is... It asks the questions how, when & where).

> ➤ <u>How</u>
>> 1) Read... but more so, Study (2 Tim 2:15 - KJV) *Study to shew thyself approved unto God, a workman that needeth not to be ashamed, rightly dividing the word of truth.* NOTE: The Greek word for Study = Spoudazo which also means Diligence.
>> 2) Prayer (Psalm 32:6) *Therefore, let everyone who is godly pray to You in a time when You may be found.* Jesus prayed to the Father

and even gives instructions on how to pray beginning in Matthew 6:9.

3) Through hearing preaching and teaching – In Romans 10:14 we're told that this is the first way to be introduced to God: *"... How will they hear without a preacher?"* For the believer - Ephesians 4:11 – 12 - *And He gave some as apostles, and some as prophets, and some as evangelists, and some as <u>pastors and teachers</u>, for the <u>equipping of the saint</u> for the work of service, <u>to the building up of the body of Christ</u>;*

➢ <u>When</u>
This is summed up in 1 Thessalonians 5:17 - *pray without ceasing. Definition of* Prayer = personal communication with God! That encompasses both talking to and listening to Him. In short... When to seek Him = ALWAYS (Without ceasing)!

➢ <u>Where</u>
In the Old Testament, the Israelites had to seek God in the Tabernacle and later, the Temple. But, in 2 Corinthians 6:16 - *For we are the temple of the living God; just as God said, "I WILL DWELL IN THEM AND WALK AMONG THEM; AND I WILL BE THEIR GOD, AND THEY SHALL BE MY PEOPLE.* Since we are the temple, we can seek Him anywhere and everywhere.

One last definition of an adverb that I didn't mention above: How Much? Deuteronomy 6:5 is known as the Shema - *You shall love the LORD your God with <u>all</u> your heart and with <u>all</u> your soul and with <u>all</u> your might.* = How much? With <u>ALL</u> of your being!

To Seek Him is to Love Him and to Love Him is to Seek Him. You'll find Him if you seek Him. He's not hiding! The truth is, He's waiting on you!

IT'S WHAT'S INSIDE
THAT COUNTS

Psalm 149:1 *Praise the LORD! Sing to the LORD a new song,*
And His praise in the congregation of the godly ones.

Worship is shown in the Bible as being very important. Yes, I understand that worship comes in many forms, but I am referring to worship in song. It surprises me how many churches downplay or minimize worship. Even Moses knew the importance of singing to the Lord. He is the author of two songs in the scriptures (Exodus 15; Deuteronomy 32 (Introduced in Deuteronomy 31:30)). NOTE: if you question the fact that they were songs; the word 'song' used in both Exodus 15:1 and Deuteronomy 31:30 is the Hebrew word, *Shiyr*, which means "song".

To further my point of its importance, we see in Revelation 15 that there is worship, in the form of music, in heaven. (I don't like to get into doctrinal differences, but, for those churches that don't believe in instruments: I have to question what they do with Psalm 150 that clearly tells us that instruments are to be used to praise God. Or Revelation 15:2, that shows that there are even instruments in heaven.)

With the importance of worship established, there is still debate over what songs are true worship songs? Should they be traditional hymns;

modern worship; contemporary worship; southern Gospel; black Gospel? The answer to that question has two parts:

First: It should meet your individual taste. What do you like that will bring you to a place where you are truly worshipping the Lord? God didn't create us all alike. Neither did He create us all with the same taste in music. Personally, I like all forms and can enter in to worshipping God with all of the above mentioned styles. However, besides catering to your taste, the songs also have to meet the second criteria.

Second: What does the song say? Does it pay homage to God? Does it tell about Him? Does it instruct as to who we should be to Him? Does it portray sound doctrine? Is it scripturally sound? If it doesn't meet these specifications, than you need to question if it is really a worship song.

Other than those two criteria, there is nothing in the Bible that tells us of God's preference in a music style. In short; He's not concerned about the packaging. An example would be like buying cereal: the box may be very colorful and fancy, but, if you don't like marshmallows and that cereal has them in it, you're not going to buy it. For cereal and for what God will accept as worship... it's what's inside that counts.

I know that often times, though, Christian music is judged by its packaging. I know those that will criticize modern worship in favor of traditional hymns. If that is what they wish to listen to, that's fine. But they need to remember that old hymns were modern worship at one time and was probably criticized by the traditionalist of that time. Truth is, they are too concerned about the packaging. Because it doesn't sound like what they would like to hear, they ignore the words and judge the packaging.

If God isn't concerned about the packaging and He tells us in Psalm 150 to, 'let _everything_ that has breath, praise the Lord', than we shouldn't judge others because their taste is different from ours.

Finally, in 2 Samuel 6, I think of how Michal judged David by the way he worshipped when bringing the Ark to Jerusalem. True... she was judging his dancing. Regardless, for my point, she didn't see his heart nor try to understand that what he was doing was before the Lord; not man. As a result, if you know the story of Michal, she was struck barren for judging David. It's the same when someone is worshipping God in song. No matter what the packaging, as long as the words are truth, it's dangerous to judge their heart or intent of worship. Don't look at the outward. It is what's inside that counts! That's what God is looking at. Also Psalm 149 says: *"Sing to the Lord a new song..."*

LYDIA FROM THYATIRA

Psalm 22:24 *For He has not despised nor abhorred the affliction of the afflicted; Nor has He hidden His face from him; But when he cried to Him for help, He heard.*

In Acts 16:1 - 12, we find Paul, Silas, Timothy and Luke travelling through Asia Minor and, thanks to a dream that God gave Paul, heading to Macedonia and the city of Philippi. In Acts 16:13 we read that on the Sabbath day they went outside the gate of Philippi to a riverside to pray. Instead, they began speaking to some women who were assembled there. In Acts 16:14 we're introduced to a woman named Lydia who was listening to Paul's message about the Lord.

So who is Lydia? Here's what we learn about her from the scriptures:

A. In Acts 16:14, we find that she was a seller of purple fabrics. Purple fabric, in those days, was a luxury and probably expensive. Since she was selling it, she was probably doing well for herself.

B. She was a worshiper of God. Although she didn't know about Jesus until hearing about Him from Paul, she still worshipped the God of the Hebrews.

C. As she was listening to Paul, God opened her heart to respond to his teachings. As a result, we find in Acts 16:15, that she became a Christian and also influenced her household to become Christians and they are all baptized.

D. She was kind and giving. She insisted that Paul and those with him lodge at her house. Since church was held in houses at that time, her house probably became the first church in Philippi and what is modern day Europe.

As I studied about Lydia, there's something else that caught my attention. We're told that she was from Thyatira; which in the Greek means affliction. The definition of affliction is; a state of pain, distress, or grief. The name Lydia, in the Greek, means to travail. The definition of travail is; pain, anguish or suffering.

Perhaps I'm reading a lot into it, but, back in those days (and also many times in the scriptures) names were given for a reason. For Lydia to have a name that means pain and to come from a town whose name means pain... Perhaps she was doing okay at this time in her life but I think that this woman had been through some hard times. (Note: In my study of the origins of that name given to her in the scriptures, there is some validity that it may very well have been given to her because of her past).

So, how does this apply to us? I feel that there are "Lydia's" who have been through much affliction (physical, mental, emotional) in every church (Note: can be a woman or a man). Yet they are still worshippers of God and love the Lord; they influence their household; they are kind and generous; they probably wouldn't mind having church in their house. As the opening verse, Psalm 22:24, tells us: God has heard their cry and has not hidden from them.

Are you a "Lydia"? If so, God bless you! Do you know a "Lydia"? If not, you should seek her/him out. There is a lot that you can glean from such a person. They are a walking testimony of how God hears us and how He helps us through our times of pain.

ME GENERATION

---

2 Timothy 4:3 – 4 *For the time will come when they will not endure sound doctrine; but wanting to have their ears tickled, they will accumulate for themselves teachers in accordance to their own desires, and will turn away their ears from the truth and will turn aside to myths.*

Narcissism, or self-centeredness, seems to be at an all-time high. My wife and I have experienced more and more people that choose to talk more and more about themselves.

On the highways, we've noticed more people tailgating (even though the person in front of them is already going over the speed limit), and cutting other people off to gain a matter of a couple of seconds in time. It's more important for them to get where they want to go rather than you and you'd better not get in their way.

It seems that the church is going the same way. There are those that want to hear only the scriptures that tell them what they can get out of Christianity rather than what they can and should do to increase the Kingdom. There are preachers and evangelists that only talk about the "happy things" in the Bible and leave out the scriptures that warn about the consequences of sin and disobedience. They are more interested in 'tickling ears' about how God can bless and will give all that one could ask for rather than speak about the Lordship of Jesus and how with every promise there's a condition. They take scriptures out of context or purposely omit those conditions. And, worse of all, they say that once a person becomes a Christian, their problems are over. I know that I've mentioned this before, but, I often wonder if they are reading the same Bible that I read?

If you continue to read 2 Timothy 4; in verse 5 Paul says, *"But you, be sober in all things, __ENDURE HARDSHIP__, do the work of an evangelist, fulfill your ministry."* Do people forget that the 12 disciples that walked here on earth with Jesus all suffered hardship? After Judas committed suicide, 10 of the remaining 11 died a martyr's death and John was exiled to Patmos. Paul, who the Lord chose to write 13 books of the Bible (Possibly 14 as some think that he may have also written Hebrews), was beheaded by the emperor Nero in Rome. John the Baptist was beheaded by Herod as a gift for his step daughter. All of these men were believers when they suffered and died. But they all went to their death for God's sake... they were selfless. If it would have been about them, they would have kept their mouth shut, and not proclaim the gospel of Jesus, to avoid dying.

Yet, there are Christians that feel that God owes them a good, comfortable and healthy life. And there are an abundance of churches that will tickle ears, as Paul prophesied, by telling them that Christianity IS all about them getting those things. Don't be one of the ones that would rather have your ears tickled, by following false doctrine, and wind up with you name not in the Lamb's Book of Life.

Yes there are blessings, but then there's life. Being about Him means that you may not always get your way or be comfortable. You may have to endure hardships and short comings. But it also means that one day, if you can endure until the end (Matthew 24:13), you will have a life of pure happiness and contentment with Him in Heaven. Don't be a part of the 'Me Generation' when it comes to your Christian walk. Instead, be a part of the 'Him Generation'.

TO SEE GOD

Job 42:5 *I have heard of You by the hearing of the ear; But now my eye sees You*

There are times in all of our lives that we have/will experience something life changing. It may be the loss of a loved one; it may be a financial collapse; it may be an illness or injury that is debilitating and permanent; it may be you having to face your own mortality. Don't think that just because you're a Christian it can't or won't happen. It happened to all of the apostles including Paul. With the exception of John, they all died at the hands of non-believers. If God didn't spare them from persecution; those that walked with and were taught personally by Jesus… who are we? Jesus Himself tells us through the Gospel of John 16:33 that in this world (life) we will have tribulations.

It also happened to King David who believed and trusted in the Lord. He brought a lot of it on himself through sin and not repenting of those sins until he was confronted by Nathan. And even after repenting, he still had to face consequences and hardships (including the death of a baby and a son that turned completely against him).

It happened, big time, to Job. We know that he was a follower of God. God was so confident in Job's faithfulness to Him that he told Satan to do anything to him but kill him and that Job's faith wouldn't falter. You know the story… Satan destroyed everything Job had: his wealth; his family; his health. Through it all, Job went through a time of mourning and having to listen to wrong counsel from his friends. But, he never blamed God (Job 1:21 – 22). Instead he blessed the name of the Lord.

With that said, I know from experience that it is easier said than done to praise God when you are going through something difficult. Even Jesus struggled in the garden at Gethsemane. He was in agony (Luke 42:44) and His sweat was like drops of blood that fell to the ground. His agony wasn't just because He knew of the physical suffering that He would have to endure. It was also of the spiritual battle that He was about to go through for the grand prize of us. He prayed to the Father, if possible, to take that cup from Him. But then he prayed for His Father's will and not His own.

We know that God's ways aren't our ways and that His thoughts are not our thoughts (Isaiah 55:8). So, when we pray for His will, we know that it may not be what we would really like to see. We simply need to trust Him. That His ways and His will for our life is perfect and has a reason.

We need to first ask God; "What are you trying to show me or teach me through this?" Then, we need to stop and reflect on our life. In doing so, God will reveal His plan… maybe not the ultimate outcome of our circumstance, but, at least, what we need to know regarding our walk. Perhaps there's sin that needs dealt with; perhaps it's how we are fellowshipping with Him; perhaps it's how we are treating others. Perhaps, as with Job in Job 42:5 (NASB), it's to truly open our eyes to see Him.

TREAT HER LIKE A LADY

Proverbs 5:18 - *Let your fountain be blessed, And rejoice in the wife of your youth.*

NOTE: So girls, as you can tell, this tidbit is primarily for men. However, it's also important for you to understand how God wants you to be treated. So... read on.

There was a song back in the early 1970's by The Cornelius Brothers and Sister Rose, titled: "Treat Her Like A Lady". Although there is a non-Christian ulterior motive conveyed in the song for, 'treating her like a lady', the title itself holds some Biblical truth.

Several years back, I felt strongly to read Hosea. As I was reading it, I came to Hosea 5:1 – 5. The chapter begins as a rebuke against Israel, Ephraim and Judah because of idol worship. Hosea 5:6 says: *"They will go with their flocks and herds To seek the LORD, but they will not find Him; He has withdrawn from them."* They were going to give their sacrifices and offerings – their tithe. The Lord couldn't be found because He didn't want to accept those offerings. Why? Hosea 5:7, *"They have <u>dealt treacherously</u> against the LORD, For they have borne illegitimate children..."* (in short, they committed adultery against God).

I had seen that word, 'treacherously' elsewhere in the Bible and it spurred my curiosity. I turned to Malachi 2:13 which tells us that the Israelites are weeping and groaning at the altar because <u>the Lord isn't accepting their offerings</u>. Malachi 2:14: *"Yet you say, 'For what reason?' Because the LORD has been a witness between you and the wife of your youth, against whom you have* <u>*dealt treacherously,*</u> *though she is your companion and your wife by covenant.* In both cases, the reference is that there is unfaithfulness (adultery against the Lord with idol worship and adultery against their wives). Do you see what God is saying here? He equates that treating ones wife wrongly is as bad as treating Him wrongly and levels the same punishment for both by not honoring tithe and offerings. Granted, the treachery here is adultery, but the implication is that He wants us to treat our wives the same as we would treat Him.

You may be asking, "Okay, so what's the big deal if God doesn't accept my offerings and what are the consequences of that?" Here's what Malachi 3:10 says: *"Bring the whole tithe into the storehouse, so that there may be food in My house, and test Me now in this,"* says the LORD of hosts, *"if I will not open for you the windows of heaven and pour out for you a blessing until it overflows."* This verse tells us that God is faithful in blessing those who tithe to Him. Yet if there is someone who tithes and gives their offerings, in abundance, and may even sacrifice their time in the Lord's service, but isn't receiving blessings, perhaps one thing that they need to do, is to reflect on how they are treating their wife. Do you really want to miss out on God's blessings!?

Maybe you don't treat your best girl treacherously but that's still not enough. There are instructions in the Bible of how you SHOULD be treating her. Those instructions can be found in Ephesians 5:25, to treat (love) her as we want Him to treat (love) us, His church. And also in 1 Peter 3:7 - *You husbands in the same way, live with your wives in an understanding way, as with someone weaker, since she is a woman; and show her honor as a fellow heir of the grace of life, so that your prayers will not be hindered.* If you're not showing your wife the honor and understanding that God instructs through those instructions, your prayers won't be answered. To me, that is even harsher than missing out on the blessings of Malachi 3:10. So, how important, to God, is the way you treat your wife? I'd answer that it is very, very important!

If you're a man and not married, but hoping to be, learn this. If you're a woman and not married, but the man you're with isn't treating you as the scriptures tells us he should, perhaps he's not God's best for you and you need to keep looking. God's best for you is going to understand God's word and want to do what He commands.

For those of you men that are married, do as Proverbs 5:18 (above) says and rejoice in your wife and then show it by treating her the way <u>God wants you to</u>… as the lady that <u>He</u> also loves and cherishes very much.

USE ME IN THE LESSER FOR THE GREATER

1 Timothy 6:6 – *But godliness actually is a means of great gain when accompanied by contentment.*

Acts 6:1 talks about the Hellenistic Jews (Jews that had lived in Greece and spoke Greek and returned to Israel). They felt slighted by Hebrew Jews. Apparently their widows were not being treated the same as the Hebrew widows.

The disciples, wanting to concentrate more on God's word rather than physically serving the people, chose what today would be considered Deacons to take care of those physical tasks of serving. (I realize that the term, 'Deacon' in some churches may be defined differently. In this instance, I'm referring to those that are ordained to do physical service in and for the church.)

Stephen stood out among those chosen. In Acts 6:5 it says that he was a man full of <u>FAITH</u> and the Holy Spirit. It's important to emphasize the word, "faith" and there is a reason that it appears before 'Holy Spirit' in that scripture. It's because of Stephen's faith that he is full of the Holy Spirit. But, even though Stephen was a man of great faith, he was given a lesser job by the disciples and he DID IT!

Because Stephen was faithful, we see the ways that God used and blessed him. Beginning in Acts 6:8 through the rest of Chapter 6 and all of Chapter 7, we see that Stephen: 1) Was given leadership; 2) Was filled even more with Grace and Power; 3) Performed signs and wonders; 4) Could hold his own against religion; 5) Was given wisdom; 6) Knew the scriptures; 7) Was martyred for Christ; 8) Was greeted personally by Christ in heaven (Hebrews 8:1 we're told that Jesus is seated on God's right hand. But, in Acts 7:55 it says that Stephen saw Jesus <u>standing</u>... Jesus was waiting to greet His servant into heaven.)

We that call ourselves Christians should all be like Stephen! To be strong in our faith and when the opportunities arise, use our God given gifts to minister; encourage; comfort; evangelize; confront and rebuke wrong teachings, etc. But we must also be willing to do the lesser jobs that need done for the kingdom. Be diligent and accept where God has placed you... even if it is doing what some may call menial. Allow God to use you as He wants... not the way you think He should. Because Stephen accepted the responsibilities given him, even serving food to the widows, God used him to confront the religious leaders of that time and to be an example even to us today.

In the 1 Timothy 6:6, above, Paul must have noticed that there were those that were using their Christianity for gain (in the context of the surrounding verses... even monetary gain). What Paul is telling Timothy: If you want gain in your life (I believe that Paul is referring more to Spiritual and ministerial gain... not worldly gain), be strong in your godliness (reverence and respect to God) and be content with where He has you now. God will do the rest. The same as He used Stephen in the lesser to eventually do something greater.

WHEN IN DOUBT

---

1 Chronicles 16:10 – 11 *Glory in His holy name; Let the heart of those who seek the LORD be glad. Seek the LORD and His strength; Seek His face continually.*

We see so many patriarchs of the faith seeking God and then God responding. However, I want to look at someone, although he sought the Lord, still had his doubts.

In Judges 6:1 - 10, we find the Midianites harassing Israel by destroying their crops and livestock. Although Israel cried out to the Lord, they were also in sin worshipping Baal. As we continue to read, we meet Gideon as an angel of the Lord visits him. (I need to make an observation here before going on: Although in Judges 6:11 it says, "an angel of the Lord"; in Judges 6:14, it says, "The Lord looked at him and said…". Many times in the Hebrew text (the old testament), when you see the term, 'angel of the Lord', the general consensus is that it is the Lord.)

In summarization (Verses Judges 6:11 – 23):

> ➤ Even though the angel addressed him as a valiant warrior, Gideon had no intentions of fighting the Midianites up to that point.
> ➤ Gideon even dares to ask as to where the Lord was during this time. He asked, "Where are the miracles?", "Why has the Lord abandoned us?"
> ➤ Gideon reminds the angel that he and his family are the least in Manasseh and he, himself, is the youngest.

- ➢ The Lord continued to encourage Gideon (Judges 6:14, 16 & 23) and not give up on him even through his doubts.
- ➢ It wasn't until Gideon prepared a meal for the Lord and saw it consumed with fire that he no longer doubted.

As we continue to read, we find Gideon doing great things for the Lord by tearing down the altars to Baal. God protected him during all of that, yet, in Judges 6:36, we see doubt start to creep in again. Now comes the story of the fleece… Gideon asks, *"If You will deliver Israel through me, as You have spoken…"* He then lays a fleece of wool on the ground and the first night asks the Lord to only allow dew to be on the fleece and not on the ground (which the Lord does). He asks on the second night to allow dew to be on the ground, but not the fleece (again, the Lord does). Now Gideon was sure that it was God. (Judges 6:37 – 40)

Have you ever doubted that God wants to use you or is even moving in your life? Have you questioned God when times were tough and you see no victory in sight? In using the story of Gideon, we can learn that it's OK to feel that way. We see that God was there all along and had great plans for Gideon even through his doubts. God was patient with him. Once Gideon felt reassured, then God, now able to use him, could be glorified (Judges 7:2).

So, even when you are wondering; questioning; doubting… don't let the enemy convince you to stop seeking God. Constantly ask God, "What's my next move?" It's also okay to pray, "Please Lord, make it clear to me!" In a sense, that is what Gideon did 3 times: Once with the meal that he prepared and twice with the fleece. Once you ask, then be patient and wait for God's answer. Even when it seems certain that you received your answer, if there is any inkling of doubt, it's OK to ask again. It's better to be certain that it's the Lord and not the enemy or your flesh.

Gideon persevered in seeking the Lord to be sure that he was doing what the Lord wanted him to do. In the opening verse (1 Corinthians 16:10 – 11 - above), it says *'let the heart of those who seek the Lord be glad'*. May you be glad always in your heart.

WHY WE GO THROUGH THINGS

Revelation 21:4 *and He will wipe away every tear from their eyes; and there will no longer be any death; there will no longer be any mourning, or crying, or pain; the first things have passed away."*

People, including Christians, have asked why God would allow us to go through tough times if He truly loves us. That's a good question and a tough question. I don't know if I have a definitive answer, but I believe that if we look at the examples in the scriptures, we can at least get a clue.

- ➤ We are not of this world (John 15:19). We have to live in this world, but we are not to be a part of it. Because we live in this world, the world is going to give us tough times. It may even hate us. But remember; it hated Jesus first. (John 15:18)
- ➤ The book of Job: We find a testimony that has spanned millennium and has encouraged and comforted innumerable others in the Lord. Our testimonies may not span as much time, but they can encourage others. Revelation 12:11 *"And they overcame him (Satan) because of the blood of the Lamb and because of the word of their testimony.* We are doing battle against the enemy when we share of how God gives us the strength to go through the tribulations in our lives and may even have brought us victoriously out on the other side.
- ➤ In Luke 7, John the Baptist, while in prison, sends his disciples to ask Jesus, *"Are you the one?"* John's faith was faltering. Jesus replied with the words of Isaiah the prophet (chapters 35:5 - 6 & 42:7)…

The blind receive sight, the lame walk, the lepers cleansed and the deaf hear. Jesus' reply didn't include Isaiah's words; *the prisoner shall be set free.* He was telling John that he was going to remain in prison. We know that John is later beheaded. John had accomplished his mission here on earth and it was time for him to go home. Unless the Lord returns first, we are all going to die (Hebrews 9:27). For the Christian, though, this isn't a tragedy. Paul says it best; Philippians 1:21 *For to me, to live is Christ and to die is gain.*

➢ Jesus' disciples knew all too well that they would also suffer. In John 21:18 – 23, Jesus prophesized Peter's death. But, when Peter asked Jesus about the Apostle John's future, Jesus' response in John 21:22; *"If I want him to remain until I come, what is that to you? YOU FOLLOW ME!"* The question is sometimes asked, why did/do I have to go through these things while others don't? Jesus' answer is… don't concern yourself about them. YOU FOLLOW ME!

➢ My final example is King David. In 2 Samuel, chapters 11 & 12, we read about King David committing adultery with Bathsheba and having her husband killed. He thought he got away with it, but, God knew and sent the prophet Nathan to confront him. After the baby was born to Bathsheba, as a result of their affair, it became sick and died. Sometimes it takes extreme measures by God to get our attention. How are we treating Him and how are we treating others? When we are going through something, we need to take a deeper look at our own lives and see if perhaps God is trying to get our attention.

Through all of our problems, God gives us a promise in Revelation 21:4 and more importantly, in verse 5, He says: *"Behold, I am making all things new".* We only need to endure for such a very short time, compared to His eternity, the sufferings we go through in this life.

WINTER BLUES

Psalm 74:17 *You have established all the boundaries of the earth; You have made summer and winter.*

During the winter months, 'Cabin Fever' starts to set in on a lot of people that live in a climate where the winters are cold, damp and icy. Thanksgiving, Christmas and New Years, help to take your mind off of the cold. However, the following months don't offer much in the way of a distraction to the weather. My wife and I have talked about being 'snow birds'. For those of you that live in a warmer climate and may not know what that means; it's usually retired people that spend the summer in their home state and then move to a warmer climate for the winter.

Although winter blues aren't fun for a lot of people, there are those that love winter. They get into winter sports; desire curling up beside a nice warm fire in the fireplace; love the beauty of a fresh snow fall.

There are benefits to winter:

> Any old timer will tell you that the cold cuts down on the bug population.
> The amount of moisture that most winters bring help to keep the water tables at a good level
> Hay fever is put to sleep along with most plants (including grass and weeds that lawn owners don't have to deal with).

The states that have a warm climate get a financial boost thanks to an increased population of snow birds and vacationers.

Yes, there are hazards in winter:

Increased risk of heart attack from shoveling snow
Icy and snowy roads create hazardous driving and an increase in serious traffic accidents.
However, there are also hazards in the other seasons:
Sun burn and over exposure to the sun that can lead to skin problems or sun stroke.
Electrical storms and tornadoes and hurricanes.
Increased insect population and devastation to crops.

Whether you love winter or hate it, there is one thing that we should all remember about it... God created it! And because He created both summer and winter, we know that they have their purpose.

We have this whole wonderful planet to live on, to laugh on, to love on, to play on. But, we also have it to cry on, go through sorrow on, die on. Yet, it's not ours. It still belongs to God... Psalm 24:1 – 2 *The earth is the LORD'S, and all it contains, the world, and those who dwell in it. For He has founded it upon the seas and established it upon the rivers.* He created the seasons to be a part of the earth.

With all of that said, the best way to solve the winter blues is to face it head on. Acknowledge that winter is a creation of God and praise Him for it. Then grab a cup of your favorite hot beverage, curl up under a blanket and enjoy a (THE) good book.

KATHY'S TIDBITS

Everyday there are moments that come our way to remind us that God is speaking, gently calling us to Himself. An invitation awaits us to see, hear and experience His presence through everyday simple life lessons. A reminder that He is always near if we will be still long enough to know that He is God.

Kathy

A LIFE LESSON FROM A CAT

Proverbs 3:5 – 6 *Trust in the Lord with all your heart, and do not lean on your own understanding; In all your ways acknowledge Him, and He will make your paths straight.*

There is a neighborhood cat (we call her Mama) that we have been feeding. She lives outside and we feed and watch over her. When the extreme weather comes in the winter, we will put her in our basement during the night. At first she was hesitant to come inside. Even in the extreme cold, she would still rather be outdoors.

One wintery night, the weather was extremely cold and the snowfall accumulated to several inches. We brought Mama inside. In the morning, we were leaving to go out of town. When it was time for us to put Mama back outside, she hesitated. The fresh fallen snow seemed too deep for her small body and she would be covered. It almost seemed impossible for her to make her own path through the snow.

Sometime during the night, another critter went through our yard and left a fresh track of footprints. Mama cat made her way to and carefully followed the ready-made trail set before her. She looked up and ahead as she made every step and it must have seemed overwhelming. But she took her time and slowly walked the path set before her without straying.

As I watched her cautiously plodding through the yard, I thought about the path that the Lord sets out for us each day. We have a choice to hear

His voice and stay on the carefully laid out course that He set before us. We should not hurry ahead on our own and think we know a better way.

Each new day presents us with fresh opportunities to influence those we come into contact with along life's journey. May we be ever mindful of the people that the Lord would have us extend His love and encouragement to. May we walk in the footsteps that Lord has made for us!

AN ORDERLY HOME AND HEART

Matthew 5:8 *Blessed are the pure in heart, for they shall see God.*

God has told me to take time to bring order to my home (A cleaning and purging of clutter and unnecessary stuff). During that process, I am thankful for what God is teaching me.

When I was a child, my family did not have very many pretty things. For mealtime, the dishes, silverware and glasses were mismatched, cracked and worn out. Mealtime was also stressful. Many times it became a free for all, between my siblings and me, in trying to get enough food on our own plates before it was gone. When I married and had my own home, I was determined to make mealtime pleasant. So I always made the food and table look inviting. I wanted mealtime to be special for us every day.

My three daughters use to tease me about how many outfits I had for our table. They would say that the table had more outfits than we did. Since I am bringing order to my home, it is finally time for me to let go of some of those table outfits. I took all of my table linens out of where they were stored and disposed of those that were worn out, stained or unwanted. Even with that purging, I am still blessed to have enough to enjoy.

Holding onto things that were no longer useful has become a burden and taken up precious space in my home. I now have space for those useful and valued items. I still set a pretty table and make yummy meals but now my focus can be more about time spent with those I love.

Through this time of getting my house in order, God is showing me that I have things in my heart that are worn out, useless and have no value. I am working on cleaning and purging and bringing order to that also. I am finding new freedom in my physical house but also in the heart that houses my God. I'm making more room for the Holy Spirit to have His way.

Our God is so patient and kind and continues to draw us closer so we can look more like Him every day. I often recite the scripture that is known as the Shema from Deuteronomy 6:4-5: *Hear o Israel! The Lord is our God, the Lord is one! You shall love the LORD your God with all your heart and with all your soul and with all your might.* My prayer is that I will love Him with <u>all</u> of my heart because it will be clean, pure and clutter free from those stained, worn out and un-needed things that took up space. And, as a result, as Jesus says in Matthew 5:8 (above), the day will come when I shall see God! I pray that for you also!

LIVE LOVED

---

1 John 3:1a (NIV) *See what great love the Father has lavished on us, that we should be called children of God! And that is what we are!*

I (Kathy) had been invited into the delivery room of my new granddaughter, who was just a few minutes old. The nurse was still taking the vitals of the baby and in my opinion was being rough on someone so small and helpless. She was holding her like a football and pulling, poking and sticking her finger in places that caused the baby to scream.

When the nurse was finished manhandling her, she handed the screaming baby off to dad and kindly said, "Here, you get to give your daughter her first bath." We all watched with tears in our eyes as dad gently took the baby in his arms. She stopped crying as he lovingly began to clean her up. He started to remove the blood and grime from her body and clean her scratches. After she was all cleaned and bundled in a warm blanket, dad just sat and stared at the beautiful baby in his arms with a smile from ear to ear. She was a part of him, safe and secure in his love because he loved her so much that he could burst.

As I observed dad cleaning up his daughter, it became a beautiful picture of God's love for His children. I was reminded of how God came, rescued me and made me a part of His family. I had been manhandled, mistreated and was bloodied and bruised by the world. He gently took me in His arms and began to clean away the debris, dirt and even the filth of the sin in my life. He wiped away my tears and blanketed me in His love.

141

He sees me as beautiful, His daughter and a reflection of Him. As I continue my journey and "grow up" in the faith, I am able to live loved knowing my Heavenly Father loves me with an everlasting love. As with the granddaughter, her father, knowing her for only a few minutes, gave his unconditional love even though she had not done anything to earn it… so my heavenly Father does with me.

If you're a believer, then you also are loved by the Father. His love is unconditional and free. In Ephesians 2:8 – 9, we are told; *For by grace you have been saved through faith; and that not of yourselves, it is the gift of God; not as a result of works, so that no one may boast.* The grace He offers is because of His love for all of us. It's not complicated… just receive that love.

In closing, here is a song that truly ministers to me about God's love for me.

"Be Loved" by Christy Nockels

THE FUNNY CIDE OF LIFE

I Corinthians 9:24 *Do you not know that those who run in a race all run, but only one receives the prize? Run in such a way that you may win (grasp, seize upon with exertion).*

During a visit to the Kentucky Horse Park while on vacation, we enjoyed a special presentation of retired horses that were once former winners of the Kentucky Derby. The trainers led out the champions one by one as the announcer read the history of each horse and their accomplishments. A small overhead TV monitor played footage of the winning races with all the fanfare and excitement.

The story of a horse named Funny Cide, who won the Kentucky Derby and The Preakness, captivated my thoughts. As he was running in the Preakness, the announcer said, "Funny Cide is stopping". That really meant he was slowing down but he still went on to win the race.

Funny Cide reminded me of a few life lessons that sunny fall afternoon:

- ➤ As followers of Jesus Christ, we are all running a race. Sometimes we pace, trot or run, but we are always moving toward the finish line.
- ➤ During the race, a horse wears blinders so they can only see what lies ahead. Oh how we need to keep our blinders on and our eyes fixed on Jesus so that we are not distracted by the busyness around us.

➤ At times it may seem as though we are stopping. But we are just taking a moment to catch our breath and check our focus so that we may continue the race set before us.

➤ Funny Cide is a fan favorite at the park and brings joy to those who come into contact with him. Although he is no longer running races, he helps in the training of younger horses. We also should help to encourage and cheer on those around us. Especially encourage the next generation to be strong in the Lord and finish the race well.

Hebrews 12:1–2 *Therefore, since we have so great a cloud of witnesses surrounding us, let us also lay aside every encumbrance (whatever is prominent, a weight) and the sin which so easily entangles us, and let us run (exert one's self, strive hard, to spend one's strength in performing or attaining something) with endurance (patiently, steadfast) the race (course full of toil and conflict) that is set before us, fixing our eyes (to turn the eyes away from other things and fix them on something) on Jesus, the author and perfecter of faith, who for the joy set before Him endured the cross, despising the shame, and has sat down at the right hand of the throne of God.*

Let us pursue the race with passion and encourage one another to finish strong dear ones!

THERE IS A CLOUD

Psalm 72:6 *May He come down like rain upon the mown grass, Like showers that water the earth.*

For several hours, dark clouds with an abundance of rain settled over our sleepy little town causing a major creek to flood. The earth, already saturated by the rain, became a lake where a playground and ballfield once were.

Schools were cancelled due to many road closures from other swelling and overflowing water ways. I saw emergency workers guarding the flooded roads from travelers that might accidently enter those dangerous areas. The workers were helpless to stop or control the flooding.

During our church service on the Sunday following those days, we sang a song by Elevation Worship titled, "There Is A Cloud". Here is a portion of that song:

> For the dry season is over
> There is a cloud, beginning to swell
> To the skies, heavy with blessing
> Lift your eyes, offer your heart
> Jesus Christ opened the heavens
> Now we receive the Spirit of God
> We receive Your rain
> We receive Your rain

As I listened to the words of the song, I could picture the water from the rain and the rising creek spilling over and pouring onto the usually dry banks. I likened it to the dry places of my heart that thirsted for more. How it was crying out to receive the rain. Then, drinking it in and Jesus renewing me with His living water.

As you journey through life, may it be with great expectation and anticipation that His presence and power will come like the flood. His fresh spring rain overflowing and, as with the emergency workers, no one can stop it (Nor would anyone want to).

Offer Him all of your heart and receive the rain of His Spirit. Allow fresh new growth to arise in your life this year.

Finally, Hosea 6:3 says: *So let us know, let us press on to know the LORD. His going forth is as certain as the dawn; And He will come to us like the rain, Like the spring rain watering the earth.*

HOLIDAY TIDBITS

I decided to group all of the holiday tidbits into one chapter, with the exceptions of Christmas, Easter and New Year's Day.

Holidays are a part of our culture. We love to have any excuse to have a day off of work and to be able to celebrate. Not that I am underplay the reason for the holiday, but those are underlying benefits of a lot of the holidays.

What I tried to do is to give us all a spiritual life lesson for each holiday, even if that holiday's roots aren't spiritually based. I even added leap year day (February 29th)... Although not designated as a holiday, it can be a time of celebration. Please don't wait until leap year to read it.

I'VE BEEN TO THE MOUNTAINTOP – MARTIN LUTHER KING JR DAY

---

1 Thessalonians 3:12 *and may the Lord cause you to increase and abound in love for one another, and for ALL PEOPLE, just as we also do for you*

On April 3rd, 1968, Dr Martin Luther King Jr., delivered the speech to the Mason Temple in Memphis, Tennessee, in which he said that he had been to the mountaintop and had seen the promised land.

Deuteronomy 34:4 tells us that the Lord took Moses up on Mount Nebo and showed him the Promised Land (The land that would become Israel). He then told Moses that he wouldn't be allowed to enter it and then Moses dies. Dr. King's vision of equality and love for all was what he was calling, "the promised land". In parallel with the story of Moses, the day following Dr. King's speech declaring that he too had seen "the promised land", April 4th, 1968, he was assassinated. Although the Lord showed Dr. King that wonderful vision, like Moses, he never got to enter that "promised land".

As Christians, it's important to the Lord that we also seek the same "promised land" that Dr. King envisioned. We hear Jesus in John's Gospel, chapters 13 and 15, repeatedly tell His disciples to, "Love one another".

The Greek word for love in all of those verses is Agapao (which is the root word of Agape; the word most associated with God's love for us). Thus, those verses (along with other verses in many of the epistles) is most commonly applied toward our love for other believers.

1 John 3:10 equates our righteousness with how we love others. If we don't practice either, than we are not of God. 1 John 4:11 – 21 continues to talk about loving one another. 1 John 4:20 says if we claim to love God and not our brother, then we are liars. (Greek – Brother = adelphos: Literal brother; same ancestry; fellow believer (brethren in Christ); ANY FELLOW OR MAN.)

The same Greek word for love (Agapao) is also used by Jesus in a different way in Matthew 5:43 – 48. In short, those verses say that we should LOVE (Agapao) our enemies. We are to demonstrate Christ's love to ALL people, (See 1 Thessalonians 3:12) and prejudice should NOT be a part of us.

Prejudices come in many forms; from skin color to nationality to political affiliation to gender to religious affiliation to sexual orientation and so on. It's OK to call sin, 'sin', if someone is living a certain sinful lifestyle. It's also OK to stand firm on our beliefs that Christ is the only way. But in all cases, we need to address those circumstances with love. If we entertain any prejudices, they should be thought of as sin. We know that God ISN'T prejudice as indicated in 1 Timothy 2:3 – 4 and 2 Peter 3:9. The word ALL is used in both of those scriptures.

We have an opportunity to go into that Promised Land that Dr. King spoke of. It boils down to whether or not we're afraid of the giants that might be there in the form of someone that might be different from us. 1 John 4:18 tells us that *there is no fear in love because perfect love casts out fear.* Cast out your fears today by knowing God's love for others. Perhaps by imitating God and demonstrating that love, you may win a soul for Christ. Be a visionary as Dr King was and not only look over into the promised land, but cross over and live there.

GROUNDHOG DAY

Matthew 6:34 - *"So do not worry about tomorrow; for tomorrow will care for itself. Each day has enough trouble of its own."*

When I think of Groundhog Day, I think of the movie with the same title starring Bill Murray. In the movie, Bill plays a narcissistic TV weatherman (Phil Connors) from Pittsburgh covering the annual Groundhog Day festivities held in Punxsutawney, Pennsylvania. He, somehow, gets caught in a time warp in which he keeps repeating the day over and over again and again. His worry is whether or not he will ever see tomorrow. February 2nd proved to be a very troublesome day for him numerous times (The number of times he repeated the day isn't specified in the movie, but it was enough that he was able to learn to play the piano very well and speak two other languages fluently.). It wasn't until he truly changed his ways and learned to care about others more than himself that the loop finally ended and he woke up on February 3rd.

Jesus tells us to not worry about tomorrow for each day has enough troubles. Unlike Phil Connors, we don't get to relive each day until we get it right. Therefore, we need to go into each day with an attitude that we are going to do our best to get it right the first time around.

To think that every day is going to be perfect, even with a positive attitude, isn't realistic. Jesus even tells us that each day has troubles. There are the unexpected happenings; the problems that we carried into the day

(IE: finances; an existing illness; unemployment; family problems); the enemies attacks. All of these things cause us to worry.

As you read through Matthew 6:25 – 32, Jesus tells us that God wants to take care of us. He doesn't want us to be consumed in worry even about our basic needs. But, as with all of God's promises, there are conditions. The condition for not worrying about tomorrow and those basic needs is found in Matthew 6:33 - *But seek first His kingdom and His righteousness;* and then what?... *all these things will be added to you.*

So, what does it mean to seek His Kingdom and Righteousness? To start, if you haven't already done so, dedicate today to the Lord and ask Him what <u>He wants you to do</u> this day (Joshua 24:15). Give Him the praise that only He deserves and worship Him (Psalm 29:2). Avoid sin and, if possible, even temptations that you may have a weakness to (Psalm 119:11). Be faithful in reading His word and keep an open line of prayer to Him throughout the day (1 Thessalonians 5:17). Don't be hesitant in laying any and ALL of your problems before Him (He wants you to). There are none too great or too small that He doesn't want you to confide in Him about (Psalm 55:22). Humble yourself. Don't be so high on yourself that you think that you think it's all about you like Phil Connors did (Proverbs 16:18). And finally, show love and compassion to others... even putting them and their needs before yours (Mark 12:33).

A last thought: As Phil Connors, when he was caught in that time warp, wasn't promised that tomorrow would ever come: Neither are we! Worrying won't change that! As Jesus says, *"And who of you by being worried can add a single hour to his life?"* So, live your life today for the Lord and whether tomorrow comes or not, it won't matter because the Lord will be there for you and with you. (Matthew 6:27)

WHOSE VALENTINE ARE YOU? – VALENTINE'S DAY

---

1 John 4:19 - *We love, because He first loved us.*

When you think of February 14th, the first thought is "Valentine's Day". It's a time when even non-romantics become sentimental. Although we've shortened it to just "Valentine's Day", it was originally called, "St Valentine's Day". But who was St Valentine and why was there a day picked to honor him and why is it associated with romance?

In researching this, I am finding that not even the church knows for sure who the real St. Valentine was. According to several sources that I used in my study, there are a possibility of at least 3 Saints named Valentine (Or Valentinus), that were all martyred in the third century. The holiday's origins did begin as a liturgical celebration and is still celebrated as an official feast day for different Christian churches of today. As for St. Valentine (whichever one of the three represents the person for whom the holiday was named) and the days association with love... that also is a mystery.

The one thing we know for sure is that it now represents a day for love to blossom and grow. My question, though; Why only one day a year? As Christians, are we not commanded to practice love always: John 13:34 – Jesus said, *"A new commandment I give to you, that you love one another, even as I have loved you, that you also love one another."* Jesus said, *"Even as I have loved you…".* His love never ceases!

That is only one of many verses that tell us about love. To understand how important this new commandment was to Jesus, we need to understand where He was and what He was considered to be.

During His ministry years, they called Jesus, Rabbi. A Rabbi, even by today's definition, is a Jewish scholar or teacher. In the time of Jesus, in Israel, that was a much respected, much esteemed position to have. Young boys were honored to be chosen by a Rabbi as his understudy. When Jesus chose His 12, they had to have been thrilled (and they were probably teen agers… not old men as modern movies portray them). Every Rabbi had his own special teaching. They would pick a commandment or something from the scriptures that was important to them and that would be their main study and teaching. For example: If you wanted to know about honoring your father and mother; that might be Rabbi Tom's specialty. So, you would go to Rabbi Tom because you would know that he would have all of the answers for you. This teaching that they specialized in was known as a Rabbi's yoke.

In Matthew 22:36, a Pharisee lawyer asked Jesus, *"Teacher, which is the great commandment in the law?"* In short, he was asking Him what His yoke was. Jesus' answer was what every Jew, let alone a Rabbi, would answer, Matthew 22:37 – 39 *"Love the Lord your God with all your heart, soul and mind. This is the great and foremost command".* What He said after that was what the Pharisee was truly inquiring about. Jesus said, *"The second is like it…"* Jesus was emphasizing that what He was about to say was just as important. He goes on to quote from Leviticus 19:18, *"… you shall love your neighbor as yourself."*

When, in Matthew 11:29 & 30 Jesus is talking about His yoke… that is what He is referring to. *"Take My yoke upon you and learn from Me, for I am gentle and humble in heart, and you will find rest for your souls. For My yoke is easy and My burden is light."*

In 1 John 4:19, the *'we love'* part means to love as Jesus teaches us to love. Don't confine it to just your love for God or those close to you. If you do, you fall short.

I know that it's not always easy to love your neighbor. However, on this day that we dedicate to love, we should practice Jesus' yoke. Please, though, don't let it be confined to just Valentine's Day. Remember Jesus' yoke year round. Remember that we are loved unconditionally (and I'm sure that I'm not always that lovable) and because of that, we should also practice that same love.

WHO'S IN CHARGE? – PRESIDENT'S DAY

---

1 Peter 2:13 – 14 – *Submit yourselves for the Lord's sake to every human institution, whether to a king as the one in authority, or to governors as sent by him for the punishment of evildoers and the praise of those who do right.*

In February the United States celebrates Presidents' Day. OK... with the exception of the closing of government offices, banks and post offices (actually, more of a nuisance if you happen to need services from any of these agencies on that date), there really isn't that big of a celebration. Presidents' Day was originally celebrated as George Washington's Birthday (February 22nd) and is still recognized as that by some government offices. Due to an act of congress in 1968 called the Uniform Monday Holiday Act, beginning in 1971, Presidents Day has been and will be celebrated on the third Monday of February regardless of the date. It is also, for the most part, considered a celebration of all presidents and not restricted to just President Washington (sorry George).

So, what's the big deal about the president? Isn't the president just another person? Yes and no! The president is a person, but, is also given authority (regardless of whether you voted for that person or not). Romans 13:1 - *Every person is to be in subjection to the governing authorities. For there is no authority except from God, and those which exist are established by God. If you* believe the scriptures and God, than you must believe that whoever is president is there because God has approved of them being there.

I brought up Romans 13:1 in a discussion with a small group of men one evening. One of the men immediately looked at me and said, "Do you really believe that God sanctioned Adolf Hitler to be a leader of Germany knowing all the atrocities that he was going to do to the Jewish people?" I couldn't answer him except to say that I believe what the scriptures tell me.

We may not always understand why God allows certain people to be in charge. I only know that His plans aren't always reveled to us. Isaiah 55:8 – 9 - *"For My thoughts are not your thoughts, Nor are your ways My ways,"* *declares the LORD. "For as the heavens are higher than the earth, so are My ways* *higher than your ways And My thoughts than your thoughts."*

There are things that our leaders do that we may not agree with, but we need to weigh the circumstances. Yes there are things that they do that we would say is sin. That's on them and the judgment of God against them. As long as we are not asked to sin, like Shadrach, Meshach and Abed-nego were ordered to do, then we need to be obedient. If they do evil, in Romans 12:19, Paul says this: *"Never take your own revenge, beloved,* *but leave room for the wrath of God, for it is written, "VENGEANCE IS MINE,* *I WILL REPAY," says the Lord."*

In Matthew Henry's* commentaries concerning Roman's 13:1, he states that Paul is saying we should be obedient for 3 reasons: First; Since God allows that person to be in power, your obedience is then subject to obeying God. Second; because of the wrath that can be brought upon you from the authorities due to disobedience. Third; Christians are scrutinized greatly as is. To go against the authority as to bring attention to yourself puts fuel on the fire for those who already have issues with Christianity.

The title of this tidbit is, "Who's In Charge?" The bottom line is that God is in charge. He's the ultimate King. In any kingdom, the King still appoints regional managers to help him over-see his subjects. For the Christian, that would be their Pastor. Yet, even pastors are subject to the authority of the land. Romans 13:2 - *Therefore whoever resists authority has opposed the ordinance of God; and they who have opposed will receive condemnation upon themselves.* You may not like who is office, but keep them in prayer... that they will follow God's principals and not the worlds. Happy Presidents Day.

Blue Letter Bible version of the Commentaries of Matthew Henry

JUBILEE – FEBRUARY 29TH – LEAP DAY

Leviticus 25:12 - For it is a jubilee; it shall be holy to you. You shall eat its crops out of the field.

If you're reading this and it is actually February 29th, than you get to celebrate an extra day this year. That's right, I said CELEBRATE!

Moses, in Leviticus 25:1 - 55, tells us of the law that God gave the Israelites concerning the Jubilee. It begins with the Lord commanding that there needs to be a Sabbath year for the land... every seventh year. On that year, you're not to plant or harvest (even if crops grow as a result of dropped seeds from previous years, you are not to reap from them). You're not to prune the grape vines nor gather the grapes. It's a year of rest for the land to honor the Lord. The Lord continues by telling Moses to tell the people that they should count off seven Sabbath years, seven times seven or forty-nine years. The fiftieth year should then be the Jubilee.

Since you have this extra day during a leap year, why not make it a day of Jubilee? Celebrate what the Lord has done for you; what He has given you; what He has promised you. As the jubilee was to be holy to the Israelites, make this day holy to you. If you have the luxury of being able to take the day off of work, than do it. Don't work around the house or do chores, but concentrate on your God.

If you do have to work, than do it heartily as unto the Lord. (Colossians 3:23 - *Whatever you do, do your work heartily, as for the Lord rather than for men.*) But, when you're not at work, dedicate that part of the day to the Lord.

So, how do you dedicate a day to the Lord?

➢ Prayer – (1 Thessalonians 5:17 – *Pray without ceasing.*)This means that you can talk to God all day. It's like having an open line to Him 24/7. On this day, though, consciously talk to Him continuously.

➢ Read the Bible –(2 Timothy 3:16 – 17 - *All Scripture is inspired by God and profitable for teaching, for reproof, for correction, for training in righteousness; so that the man of God may be adequate, equipped for every good work.*) Let this be a day of equipping yourself to do God's work. In short, a day to make ready for the future work that you will do for the Lord.

➢ Pay special attention to your family – (1 Timothy 5:8 - *But if anyone does not provide for his own, and especially for those of his household, he has denied the faith and is worse than an unbeliever.*) Since the main point in 1 Timothy 5 beginning in verse 3, is to provide for widows, in context, this is a rebuke by Paul for those that weren't even providing for their own family members let alone the widows of the community. The Greek word used for *"Provide"* in the verse is, "Pronoeo". Yes, it means provide for; but it also means to care for; to take thought for. Let this be a day where you give extra care and extra thought to your family.

➢ If the opportunity arises on this day, show Christ's love to others (Co-workers; neighbors; even strangers) (John 13:34; 15:12 & 17 Jesus commands – *"...that you love one another"*)! Whenever Jesus says something once, it's important. Whenever He says something 3 times and the scriptures refer to it 18 more times (NASB), it's really important. You just may have to swallow your pride on this one by showing love to someone you may not have the best of relations with.

➤ Rest – (Matthew 11:29 – *Take My yoke upon you and learn from Me, for I am gentle and humble in heart, and YOU WILL FIND REST FOR YOUR SOULS.*)See Matthew 22:37 – 40 - If you show Christ's love, then you find rest.

There's nothing difficult about doing any of the above things to celebrate your own day of jubilee to pay honor to God.

ST. PATRICK'S DAY

Psalm 40:4 *Blessed is the one who trusts in the LORD, who does not look to the proud, to those who turn aside to false gods.*

The celebration of St Patrick's Day is in memory of the alleged date of St. Patrick's death; March 17th.

Although Christianity may have been introduced prior, St. Patrick is usually given the credit of evangelizing Ireland sometime in the 5th century A.D. There is a lot of legend that accompanies this patron saint of the Emerald Isle, so it is difficult to distinguish fact from fiction. Most commentaries do believe that St. Patrick was not Irish. Instead he was born somewhere else in the British Isles, (then under Roman rule) perhaps Scotland. Legend has it that, in his mid-teens, he was captured by pirates and sold into slavery in Ireland where he tended sheep. After several years of captivity, he escaped and returned to his family. He then joined the priesthood and felt a calling to go back to Ireland and share the gospel. Prior to that, most of Ireland practiced Celtic polytheism = having many gods of Celtic origin.

There are a few things that stand out to me about this man (providing that the core of who he was, is correctly represented through history despite the legendary acclaims):

First: That he wasn't influenced by the false religions that he grew up with. The fact that Brittan was under Roman rule, Roman gods would have been openly worshipped where he grew up. For the years he was in captivity, in Ireland, he would have then been exposed to the Celtic Gods. (SIDENOTE: We also are exposed to false gods that we may not even recognize as gods... IE: money or riches, celebrities, sports teams, people that we elevate (including loved ones or clergy) and even our jobs. The way we make them gods is by putting more trust in them then we put in the one true God.)

Second: That he chose to not only worship the God of the Bible, but he decided to commit his life to serving Him.

Third: That he went back into a region that was steeped in false religion to try and bring those people to the truth of Jesus.

Follow St. Patrick's example:

1) Don't give in to those false gods but instead fervently proclaim your faith in Jesus.
2) Find a way to serve Him. As James says; (2:26), *"Faith without works is dead."*
3) Do the work of an evangelist (2 Timothy 4:5) and share Him with the unsaved.

One final thought: Although I give St. Patrick credit for his accomplishments, it's important to not put him or any other person too high on a pedestal. As it says in Psalm 40 (above), Saint Patrick is blessed for his trust in the Lord and by not turning to false gods. But give the true honor and glory for the day that bears St. Patrick's name, to the Lord, Jesus Christ. After all, He's the one that created St. Patrick, Ireland, the color green, you and me and the day.

DON'T BE FOOLED – APRIL FOOL'S DAY

Matthew 5:22 *But I say to you that everyone who is angry with his brother shall be guilty before the court; and whoever says to his brother, 'You good-for-nothing,' shall be guilty before the supreme court; and whoever says, 'You fool,' shall be guilty enough to go into the fiery hell.*

I have had many April Fools jokes played on me. I have to admit, I have also played a few on others. But if you think of what that term, April Fool, means; by catching someone with a prank or a joke, you're calling them a fool because they fell for it.

In Matthew 5:22 (above), Jesus says if you call someone a "fool," you're in danger of Hell. That seems pretty tough. If we break the verse down, we can see why it seems tough and what He is really saying.

Jesus uses the term, 'Brother,' to identify the person receiving the anger and insults.

Brother - Greek = Adelphos. Definition (best fit) is a fellow believer or brethren in Christ.

Jesus is saying that God doesn't appreciate when His children are mean to each other. It goes to the extent that, even though you may be one of His children, there is punishment levied. What about the punishment?

If you're angry, then you're guilty before the court.

'Before the court' – Greek = Krisis = judgement (usually from lesser courts) – you're going to be judged for your anger towards your brother. Not judgement to death, but still a judgement.

If you call someone, 'Good for nothing,' then you are guilty before the Supreme Court.

'Good for nothing' - Greek = Rhaka = empty one or worthless. To God none of us are worthless.

'The Supreme Court' - Greek = synedrion = the Sanhedrin – the main governing body in those days made up of important people including some Pharisee's. They could sentence one to prison or even death.

But to call someone a 'Fool'… that could mean going to Hell.

Fool – Greek = Moros = foolish, impious, godless – also: an act or appointment of God is deemed foolish by men; despising that which relates to salvation. Although the word, moros, is translated fool, in fact, it's more about judging that brother's/sister's heart. Jesus tells us in Matthew 7:1 & 2, we're to judge not or we will be judged by the same measure. It's not our place to judge the heart. To do so is to play God and we're not Him. Satan wanted to be God and it got him cast into Hell. The thing that strikes me the most is that, according to Jesus, if we do that, we are already guilty. There's no trial.

With all of that said, I don't feel that playing a joke on someone on April Fool's Day will endanger you to be cast into Hell. However, it is important that we do watch our tongue and how we look at and even judge other believers. Jesus' yoke is to love the Lord your God with all your heart, soul and mind and, to love your neighbor as you love yourself (Matthew 22:37 – 39).

Don't you be a fool. Practice the love of Jesus with everyone that you meet. Remain guiltless in this.

MEMORIES – MEMORIAL DAY

Proverbs 10:7a *The memory of the righteous is blessed,*

It's around this date that we, in the United States, celebrate Memorial Day. Memorial Day is a commemoration of members of the U. S. Armed Forces that died during wartime. The last Monday in May is set aside for this holiday although prior to 1971 it was always celebrated on May 30th.

When I was a volunteer fireman, there were several Memorial Day mornings that I would take part in the proceedings to honor those soldiers from the small village I grew up in. All of us firemen would have our dress uniforms on and, at a designated time, we would march from the fire hall to a little church about a quarter of a mile away. Sitting in a grassy area at the corner of the church property was a granite memorial with the names of all the soldiers that had lived in the village and served in the military during war time. The firemen would line both sides of the small walkway leading up to the memorial. As the name of an organization, from the community, was read from a list, individuals representing those organizations would proceed, one at a time, up the walkway and place a basket of flowers at the base of the memorial. My last couple of years with the fire department, I took over the chaplaincy and would read a pre-scripted memorial prayer at the proceedings. To close the ceremony, there was a 21 gun salute and "Taps" were played on a trumpet with a second trumpet playing an echo somewhere behind the tiny church.

Although I didn't know all of the names on that granite memorial, I would tear up of the thoughts of the men and women who gave their all for something that they believed in. Even though they weren't there to see or hear it, this was a way of blessing them by remembering what they did for the rest of us.

What about the memories of those that have fought the spiritual battles... Who have given their all in the name of Christ?

I remember the person that I call my spiritual mother. I remember the day that she gave her life to the Lord. Her son, who lived several states away and was an evangelic minister, was visiting her. He witnessed to his mother and prayed with her to receive Jesus. He then baptized her in her own bathtub in her basement. I was there but stayed in her living room watching TV. I wasn't a believer at the time and didn't really want anything to do with that, "cultish" stuff. When she came up out of the water, the TV wasn't loud enough nor were there enough floors between us for me not to hear her shouts of praise to Jesus. (Understand something: I can truthfully testify that was not her prior to that moment. She had a true Holy Spirit experience). At some point, she sent my wife, that was there witnessing the baptism, upstairs to get me. She told her to tell me that, "Jesus wants me to come to Him and He wants to use me!" I said, "No way!" and went out and jumped on my motorcycle and left. Little did I know then how prophetic her words were on that day.

For several years following that, my mother-in-law witnessed to me. When my first wife wanted to leave me, I didn't know which way to turn. I then remembered how my mother-in-law would often share with me that Jesus loves me and would <u>never leave me</u> (Hebrews 13:5 (KJV)). As a result, it was then that I went to her and she led me to Him.

She has since gone on to be with the Lord. I still think of her influence on my life and its roll in me becoming a believer. What a blessing those memories of her are to me.

Are there close spiritual brothers and/or sisters that you know that have gone on to be with the Lord? What memories do you have of them? When you remember them, are you blessed?

Another question to ask yourself: When you die, will those left behind be blessed with memories of you? If it's tough to answer that in a positive way, it's not too late to start to leave a legacy that will bless them. If you feel that they will be blessed, then increase those blessings by giving them even more good memories.

INDEPENDENCE – 4TH OF JULY

Psalm 102:19 – 20 *For He looked down from His holy height; From heaven the LORD gazed upon the earth, To hear the groaning of the prisoner, To set free those who were doomed to death*

Unlike other holidays that are under the Uniform Monday Holiday Act, Independence Day is celebrated every year on July 4th; regardless of the day of the week. It's a day when the United States of America celebrates its breaking away from British rule back in 1776. As a nation, we wanted freedom to govern ourselves. Great Britain was the most powerful nation in the world at that time and we wanted to separate ourselves from being ruled by that great kingdom and its king; King George III. While under the rule of King George, we were almost slaves… working to pay off Great Britain's debts. The taxation was incredibly high and we had no say or representation in return. We didn't have a voice to even enter our petitions to the king.

There seems to be a little irony in the fact that as Christians, we want to be a part of an even greater <u>Kingdom</u>. We also love and admire our King (unlike King George) for setting us free. Yet, with Jesus, our debts have been paid in full and we don't need a representative; we can go right to the King with our thoughts and prayers. The only thing He requires of us is our love and devotion to Him.

Neither are we slaves in His kingdom. Galatians 5:1 *It was for freedom that Christ set us free; therefore keep standing firm and do not be subject again to a yoke of slavery.* And, even though we were once slaves to sin and death, they no longer loom over us… Romans 8:2 *For the law of the Spirit of life in Christ Jesus has set you free from the law of sin and of death.*

Hopefully, you know this freedom and independence that Jesus offers. That's right, independence. We are free to do as we please. But, because of our love and devotion to our King, we want to do what is right and what pleases Him. Yes, there are times we struggle. Even Paul confesses, *For the good that I want, I do not do, but I practice the very evil that I do not want.* (Romans 7:19) Even though there are times we do struggle, we are still under God's grace. (Ephesians 2:8) Take caution though; grace doesn't give us a license to carelessly abuse that independence. Paul also says in Romans 6:15 *What then? Shall we sin because we are not under law but under grace? May it never be!*

So, on July 4th, as the United States celebrates its independence from being ruled by a now dead king, let us celebrate our freedom of being under the Lordship of a living, powerful, yet loving King. *"So if the Son makes you free, you will be free indeed."* (John 8:36)

THEY THAT DON'T LABOR IN VAIN – LABOR DAY

Psalm 127:1 Unless the LORD builds the house, They labor in vain who build it;

On the first Monday in September, we, in the USA, celebrate Labor Day. Labor Day is a day set aside to honor the workers of America and the contributions that they have made to grow this nation in its independence and strength. It also brings most of us into the reality that this is summers last hooray and time for children to return to school. So, most people make the best of it with picnics, family gatherings or just taking it easy. Although it is called Labor Day, there is very little labor involved.

We, as Christians, are also called to labor so as to grow, not a physical nation, but a spiritual kingdom; God's kingdom. As in Psalm 127:1, above, it says, *"unless God builds the house"* (He is the architect); *"They labor in vain who build it"* (We are His laborers). We need to follow His blueprints and we will be fruitful in our labors.

Know that there is no shortage of labor; but a shortage of laborers. *And Jesus was saying to them, "The harvest is plentiful, but the laborers are few; therefore beseech the Lord of the harvest to send out laborers into His harvest."* (Luke 10:2) What labor are you called to?

The scriptures give us examples of different jobs available in God's 'Help Wanted' ad. Read them and then see which position(s) you may qualify for as per the gift(s) that God has given to you. If you're not sure where to look, here are a few examples:

Ephesians 4:11 & 12 is a good place to start: *And He gave some as apostles, and some as prophets, and some as evangelists, and some as pastors and teachers, for the equipping of the saints for the <u>work of service</u>, to the <u>building up of the body of Christ</u>.*

Romans 10:14 & 15 tells about evangelizing and missions. I love how in verse *15*, Paul is referring to Isaiah 52:7 when he says: *"HOW BEAUTIFUL ARE THE FEET OF THOSE WHO BRING GOOD NEWS OF GOOD THINGS!"* Doing God's labor is a beautiful thing.

Perhaps you don't feel as though you verbalize well and you would do better with hands on work. An example of this type of labor for the kingdom is found in Acts 6:5. Several, including Stephen, are chosen by the disciples to wait on tables and do physical labor for the body.

Within your own church, it's important to be involved. I'm sure if you ask your pastor for something to do he won't hesitate in finding you a place that will suit you.

As stated above, your labor should be in accordance with the gift(s) that God has given you. In 1 Corinthians 12 beginning in verse 4, we're told that there are a variety of gifts, but all given by the same Spirit (the Holy Spirit); there are a variety of ministries, guided by the Lord, to be a laborer in; there are a variety of effects (NASB - work to be done for the Kingdom) but one God distributing that work. 1 Corinthians 12:8 through 10 lists several gifts, but 1 Corinthians 12:7 and 11 tell us that it's the Holy Spirit that distributes the gifts as needed. In short, not everyone will have the same gifts but when we labor together, it serves the common good for the Kingdom. (Example: in construction, there are electricians, plumbers, carpenters, masons, HVAC techs, etc. Each person with their own particular skill (gift) will work on that portion of the building... but, while working together, it becomes a house.)

In accordance with the national holiday, let us, Christians, also celebrate the labor that we have done and the things accomplished for our King. But, let's also not get so comfortable that we give the enemy a crack to enter in. Seek the Lord constantly for guidance and then use your gifts and talents to <u>continue</u> to build His Kingdom as <u>He directs</u>. Don't allow your labor to be in vain.

ALL HALLOWS EVE

Philippians 4:8 *Finally, brethren, whatever is true, whatever is honorable, whatever is right, whatever is pure, whatever is lovely, whatever is of good repute, if there is any excellence and if anything worthy of praise, dwell on these things.*

I loved trick or treating when I was a child. I wasn't a Christian (although I did go to church… I hadn't made a commitment to Jesus). I know that I wore various costumes over the years, but I can only distinctly remember one. I went dressed up as a robot. My dad took a sizable box and painted it silver. He then turned it upside down, with the open end down. He cut a hole for my head to go through, on what was now the top, and arm holes on either side. He then took a smaller box and cut out eyes and a mouth and glued the open end of it over the hole that was cut in the top of the bigger box. It turned out to be very cumbersome and hard to navigate narrow passageways, such as gates. I was always of a small build and because of that, it slid around on me to where it was a chore for me to keep the eye holes lined up so that I could see where I was going. To top it all off, we wound up getting an early snow that year on Halloween night making it slippery. Never the less, I remember enjoying it immensely.

For most children, at least from my generation, that is what we remember about Halloween. It had nothing to do with trying to be extra frightening or evil looking. Nor was it about worshipping the devil. It was about dressing up and having fun going out to get candy. It wasn't until I became a Christian, when I was in my thirties, that I learned the origins of Halloween and some of the real evil that does go on during that time of year. If you don't know Halloweens true origins, then take some time to study them. Although a mainstream church has made that night a religious holiday, known as All Hallows Eve or All Saints Eve, there isn't much that is holy about the history of that night.

In Philippians 4:8 (above), it tells us of the things we are to dwell on. Here's a comparison of that verse and what Halloween night really represents:

> True – The night is a special night for Satanist. Satan is the father of <u>lies</u> not truth (John 8:44).
> Honorable – We're to hold God in high honor (1 Timothy 6:13 – 16). Halloween honors the wicked.
> Right –God is righteous and loves those that do right (Psalm 11:7). Halloween is about doing evil.
> Pure – There is nothing pure about wickedness and evil.
> Lovely – It seems that the more grotesque and ugly something is, the more that night embraces it.
> Of Good Repute – This means to have a good reputation. What kind of reputation do witches and demons represent?
> Excellence – There is nothing excellent about wanting to scare others or patronize darkness over light.
> Worthy of Praise – When you are partaking in something with an evil background, it's not worthy of praise.

If we call ourselves Christians and want to represent Christ, than we do need to be careful in what we partake in, or at least, how we partake in it. Luke 11:35 Jesus said - *Then watch out that the light in you is not darkness.* If you want to take your children out trick or treating on that night, than, at least, dress them up as Biblical characters or something that doesn't represent the evil of that night. Also, if you choose to give out treats, one suggestion I have, and that I have done in the past, is to pass out tracts with the treats. As a child, I remember receiving a Chic Tract one Halloween and reading it... numerous times. Even as a child, it made me think.

We're called to be a light in this dark world. One way to do that is by not participating in things associated with darkness. If you find it necessary to have your children participate in something, I know of churches that have harvest parties instead; where the children dress up like Bible characters or farm animals. Find one in your area or, better still, talk to your pastor about your church doing something like that. Share the light… not darkness.

HONOR TO OUR VETS
– VETERAN'S DAY

Romans 13:7 - *Render to all what is due them: tax to whom tax is due; custom to whom custom; fear to whom fear; honor to whom honor.*

November 11th, in the United States, is designated as Veterans Day; a day set aside to pay tribute to all those that have served in the US military... especially during war time.

My wife, Kathy, works for a Christian school as a secretary. There are times that the school has special programs. When they do, it seems as though they always need help with something or other. My wife, eager to want to help in some way, likes to volunteer me and then tells me, after the fact; "By-the-way, I said that you would help out with..." One of those times that I was volunteered was for a Veterans Day program that the school does annually. They invite many veterans and they needed a golf cart driver to drive some of the vets, who have difficulty walking, between the church and the school cafeteria for a luncheon following the program. Since my services weren't needed until after the ceremony, I was able to sit and watch the tribute.

What a wonderful tribute it was. The different age groups of students got up and sang patriotic songs; there was a touching poem read about a grown child's perspective of her aged father who was a war veteran; a local county commissioner, who was himself a vet, gave a tribute speech; the school band played the various themes of the different branches of the U.S. military and the vets in the audience were encouraged to stand when the theme of the branch that they had served in was played; a bagpiper played Amazing Grace; the pastor of the affiliated church gave a good short and to the point gospel message. At the end, the veterans were asked to come forward and stand in front of the stage so that as the children exited, they could shake their hands and thank them for serving. There were many tears shed during the ceremony. How wonderful it was to be able to pay tribute to those that served.

We have a wonderful freedom in this country. We are still allowed to worship our God and attend such programs. There are many countries in the world where people are openly persecuted (even killed) by just mentioning a god (or at least one that is different from the one that their government supports). We have this freedom because there are men and women who have laid their life on the line for that reason. Some have paid the ultimate price leaving a grieving family behind. Some have returned much different than when they left... physically and/or mentally.

In the opening scripture out of Romans, we are told to give honor to those that it is due. We don't have to agree with all of the politics involved, but we should be grateful and pay honor to those that have served and that are presently serving in the U.S. military. There may come a time when the luxury of being able to read a Bible; pray to our Lord; gather together in His name, will be taken from us. But for now, and since the time this country was formed (in part, for religious freedom), let us thank those that have made it possible.

I know that some of you may struggle with the 'killing' aspect the military. You may ask, "Do some of these vets have blood on their hands?" My response is to ask: what about Abraham; Moses; David and other patriarchs of the Bible that killed? It's easy to say that God sanctioned those wars. Is it possible, so that you and I can have the joy of being able to freely worship Him, that perhaps some of our wars were sanctioned also? Even if you struggle with the killing aspect, forgive as God forgives.

According to Mark 3:28 – 29 all sins are forgivable with the exception of blaspheme of the Holy Spirit.

If you know a veteran, thank him or her today. As you do, it may also give you an opportunity to encourage them in the Lord, if they are a Christian, or to witness to them about your God if they are not.

A LETTER TO AUNT ROSE
- THANKSGIVING

John 16:33 *"These things I have spoken to you, so that in Me you may have peace. In the world you have tribulation, but take courage; I have overcome the world."*

My wife Kathy had an aunt that always treated her special. Aunt Rose was well to do and lived in a retirement community in Florida. One year, in the fall, we received word that her breast cancer had returned and had metastasized even though she had a mastectomy several years earlier. Although she was receiving treatments, the prognosis wasn't good. Kathy and I had often spoken to her about the Lord and prayed with her, but, her spiritual condition was also in question. It was the day before Thanksgiving of that year that I felt compelled to send her an email. The following are excerpts from that email:

> *Aunt Rose,*
> *Too bad you're not closer. We would love to celebrate the day with you and have you over for Thanksgiving dinner.*
>
> *Kathy has kept me informed of your health. I pray that you aren't suffering much pain; both physical and emotional. We have a mighty God that loves us very much. With that said,*

I know people who would say, "If He loves us so much, why would He allow us to go through such things?"

My reply to that is scriptural; In the Gospel of John - 16:33 - Jesus said, "In this world, you <u>will</u> have tribulation. But, be of good cheer for I (Jesus) have overcome the world." In short, we are just passing through this world and this life is short compared to God's eternity. By putting all of our faith and trust in Jesus, we're guaranteed a better life beyond this world which will last for that eternity. So many people get caught up in the things of this life and lose sight of that. Jesus tells us to not worry about things of this world, but think on things eternal.

I use the following analogy as an example to describe God's eternity: If you take a grain of sand and look at its molecular form, I don't think it is unrealistic to think that the grain of sand might be made up of a million molecules. If each molecule represented 1 year, than the grain of sand would represent a million years. Now, think of how many grains of sand there are on the earth; in every desert, on every beach, even in every child's sand box. Take all of those grains of sand on the earth and add those years together - That would just be the beginning of God's eternity. <u>If we spend that eternity with God</u>, the Bible tells us that it will be bliss. The book of Revelation (21:4) says, there will be no more crying, no more death, no more pain - only the joy of the Lord.

I know that this may be a scary time for you, but, know that if you trust that God doesn't make bad decisions and put your faith in Him no matter what, He'll see you through it. He doesn't promise a healing, although He is very capable of doing that. He does promise that He will give you a peace that passes all understanding <u>if you let Him</u>.

I pray that you find that peace during this time. I just wanted
to encourage you and let you know that you are being prayed
for and we care about you and love you very much.
Paul

What are you going through today? Sickness? The loss of a loved one? Financial difficulties? Does it seem as though the Lord isn't there? Let me reassure you; He is! No, you may not be getting the answer from Him that you desire. But, remember: we are just passing through this life. Jesus, Himself, tells us that we are going to have problems in this world. But then He says, *"be of good cheer"*... there is so much better waiting for us!

Aunt Rose came to spend her last couple of months near us, before dying, by living with Kathy's niece. We visited frequently and every time before we would leave, she asked that we pray together. I know she was still afraid, but, she was able to feel a peace through those prayers. I pray that you will find your peace today in the Lord, Jesus Christ.

GIVE THANKS - THANKSGIVING

Philippians 4:6 (KJV) *Be careful for nothing; but in every thing by prayer and supplication with thanksgiving let your requests be made known unto God.*

Although I had done some inter-city missions work in New York City, my first mission trip to a different country was Mexico. A few people at our church had met a former YWAM leader. His ministry was to take small groups from churches into different countries and introduce them to missions. Our church decided to have him lead a team which I became a part of.

Our destination was Cancun Mexico. Okay, I know what you might be thinking, but let me explain. When Cancun started building its tourist area, people pulled up stakes and moved there from all over Mexico hoping to get a job. The estimate was that over a million people made the migration. Unfortunately, there were only a couple of thousand jobs to be had. Most of the people that made the trek were stuck there. They had spent all of their money to get to Cancun and had nowhere else to go. Using whatever materials they could find, the jobless built make shift homes… thousands of them. They are buried in an area of Cancun that tourists don't see.

We would go into those areas and set up our puppet stage. We would do worship songs using the puppets. We would also do wordless skits or dramas telling of God's love. All the while, we battled mosquitoes, raw sewage in the streets with its stench and heat and humidity.

The children and adults that came out to see us also battled those same conditions along with the fact that they lived in poverty and may not have known where their next meal would come from. Yet, with all of those adverse things, the one thing that caught my attention above everything else is that they sang along with the puppets... they laughed and truly enjoyed themselves. They paid close attention to the skits and dramas that told of Jesus and of His love and forgiveness. They prayed when we prayed... some to receive the Lord and His salvation. Even though they had every right to feel sorry for themselves and express that to us... very few did. In most locations, not even one person did. Many, instead, thanked us for coming and sharing our time with them.

As we are celebrating Thanksgiving in this nation of abundance, be thankful for what you have. Even if this is a time in your life when thankfulness and joy are hard to fathom because of trials or tribulations, give it over to God as stated in Philippians 4:6, above. Do so with a thanksgiving that He is your God and cares for you and loves you even during this time. The result of doing that is found in the next verse: Philippians 4:7 (KJV) *And the peace of God, which passeth all understanding, shall keep your hearts and minds through Christ Jesus.*

The impoverished people of Cancun were able to experience joy and peace even while experiencing life at a low that most of us can't even imagine. Know that kind of joy and experience His peace. As you do so, truly give Him the thanks that only He deserves.

NEW YEAR TIDBITS

These are 2 tidbits dealing with entering a new calendar year. These tidbits are to encourage, but to also help us all to commit to a better walk with God in the coming year. With that said, you can wait until December 31st and January 1st to read them (I dated them so that everyone will know which tidbit is for which day). However, even if it's not close to New Year's Day, you can still read them and make the suggested commitments from that period of time forward.

Happy New Year!

OUT WITH THE OLD

Luke 5:37 *"And no one puts new wine into old wineskins; otherwise the new wine will burst the skins and it will be spilled out, and the skins will be ruined."*

I think most would agree that old habits are hard to break. As for the need to break those habits… it depends on whether they are bad habits; habits that might not necessarily be bad, but neither are they of any benefit; or they are good habits.

As Christians, we are supposed to be a new creature (2 Corinthians 5:17). That means that when we accepted Christ and gave our lives over to Him, there was a change in us. Our soul that was condemned to die and was, in fact, already dead, was brought to life. There was a change of attitude and an outlook on life itself. We received the Holy Spirit and as Paul tells us in Galatians 2:20, *"…it is no longer I who live, but Christ lives in me;"*.

Following that initial commitment, though, there is a growing process. The scriptures speak for themselves. Ephesians 4:11 (KJV) *And He gave some, apostles; and some, prophets; and some, evangelists; and some, pastors and teachers.* Why? Ephesians 4:12 – 13a *For the perfecting of the saints, for the work of the ministry, for the edifying of the body of Christ: Till we all come in the unity of the faith, and of the knowledge of the Son of God…*

It's important to grow in the faith and be perfected. From that, if you're not yet, you can be chosen by God to be one of those mentioned in Ephesians

4:11 (KJV). One of the ways to start is by keeping and even strengthening your good spiritual habits (IE: reading and studying the scriptures; praying; attending church regularly; sharing the Word wherever you go; so many more.). Another way is by shedding the bad habits; both spiritual and fleshly (IE: foul language and/or course jokes; giving in to pier pressure to do things that aren't pleasing to the Lord; watching too much television and not reading the Bible or praying enough; arguing, fighting, gossiping and being bitter towards others; so many more.).

As this year is ending, end those bad habits. Decide today that you are going to start new tomorrow in your walk and commitment to God with new good habits. As Jesus said, in Luke 5:37, above, don't put your new self in an old package. It won't work. It will be the old that will cause the new to be lost.

Jesus knew that it was a hard thing to do though. In Luke 5:39 He says: *"And no one, after drinking old wine wishes for new; for he says, 'The old is good enough.'"* Don't settle for the old being 'good enough'. As Paul says in 1 Corinthians 13:11 *"When I was a child, I used to speak like a child, think like a child, reason like a child; when I became a man, I did away with childish things."* Do away with the childish things of old and let the coming year be one of adulthood; of a new wine in a new vessel; of a new you basking in God's glory and presence like you've not yet experienced. Out with the old (be honest with yourself… you know what that should be) and in with the new.

A NEW BEGINNING

Psalm 30:5 - *For His anger is but for a moment, His favor is for a lifetime; Weeping may last for the night, But a shout of joy comes in the morning.*

With the celebration of a new year comes a new beginning. There are times that we need a relevant point in time to make changes. Let's make the beginning of a new year be that point in our lives. Let this be our new morning; but not for a day… let it, instead, be a morning for the rest of our earthly lives. Let us begin shouting joyfully for our God throughout the day, every day.

In the past year, you may have had sorrow, strife, contention, anger and/or disappointment. The source of these troubles in our lives may come from attacks from the enemy; health issues; attacks of our own flesh; attitudes that we choose; attitudes of others towards us. To find joy in these times is tough to do. We feel that when there's order in our lives (when none of the above listings are issues in our lives) then we can have joy. To find peace… that's different. So many people equate Order to Peace and that's not always the case.

When my wife and I were in Egypt on a teaching tour, we learned the difference between the two. The Israelites were content in Egypt, at least at first, because there was order. They felt like it was peace but they were straying from the God of their fathers. The land that they knew was a lush, green, plentiful land of true milk and honey. Every year, the Nile would flood and once the waters receded the ground was fertile and able to provide abundance. The Israelites flourished. However, it says in Exodus 1:8, *"There was a new king over Egypt, who did not know Joseph."* Once that king and the sub-sequential kings came to power, things began getting harder and harder on the Israelites. The order, that had once brought them joy that was Egypt, was still there. However, the trouble for God's chosen increased. The children of Abraham needed Shalom (peace) not order.

Out of the floods in our lives, we try to make order. That's not what Jesus promises though. John 16:33b - Jesus said; *"In this world, you will have tribulation. But be of good cheer, for I (Jesus) have overcome the world."* Jesus is saying that He doesn't promise order. But, if we would just trust in Him, He does promise Shalom.

In this new year, learn to trust in the peace from God, not the order of Egypt. As you walk with the Lord in that Shalom, order may come. But, even if it doesn't, you will still have His peace to comfort you and guide you and help you to get through it.

Philippians 4:7 (KJV) is a promise from God: *"And the peace of God, which passeth all understanding, shall keep your hearts and minds through Christ Jesus."* But, Philippians 4:6 (KJV) tells us our part in that: *"Be careful for nothing; but in every -thing by prayer and supplication with thanksgiving let your requests be made known unto God."* Turn everything over to Jesus - EVERYTHING! Your life first, if you haven't already done so. Give Him your troubles, sorrows and even your good times with Thanksgiving (Thanking Him that He is your God and that He is in control). And, I think it's important to mention, it's not just in words. It has to also be in attitude.

In short, believe that He hears you and that He is doing a work in you and for you when you pray. That's when peace will come. A peace that truly does pass all understanding and a morning like joy for all eternity.

May this new year bring you that peace and as a result… joy in the Lord!

EASTER AND PASSOVER TIDBITS

Since Easter (or Resurrection Sunday, as some would rather call it) and Passover fall around the same time each year, I've combined this section to include tidbits about both of those holidays.

There are probably some that are reading this that question as to why I would even include Passover, asking the question, "Isn't that a Jewish holiday?" If you read the included tidbits that talk about Passover, you'll understand. Also, I am sure that there may be some Messianic readers who still celebrate the Passover.

Kathy and I have had the opportunity to celebrate Passover in the past. We would love to do it more often because it is such a wonderful celebration of God's power, mercy and faithfulness to His people (Which now includes us Christians (Galatians 3:29). It also is very prophetic about our Lord, Jesus. As a result, my prayer is that perhaps some of our Jewish friends will read this and, as a result, recognize Jesus as the Messiah.

GOOD FRIDAY

Luke 23:42 *And he was saying, "Jesus, remember me when You come into Your kingdom!"*

In Luke 23:32 & 39 – 43, we read about the two thieves that were crucified at the same time as the Lord. I love the parallels portrayed through that event:

Luke 23:32 - *Two others also, who were criminals, were being led away to be put to death with Him.* We are criminals (sinners). Romans 3:23 tells us that *all have sinned.* Those crimes are worthy of our spiritual death. But, when we walk with Christ, His death, on that day, gives us life.

Luke 23:39 - *One of the criminals that was being crucified with Him was hurling abuse at Him, saying, "Are You not the Christ? Save Yourself and us!"* In my BC days (before I came to Christ) I used His name in vain. I doubted Him. I would mainly pray when I was in trouble and needed His help. I also had problems understanding why He would allow bad things to happen (especially to me).

Luke 23:40 & 41 - *But the other answered, and rebuking him said, "Do you not even fear God, since you are under the same sentence of condemnation? And we indeed are suffering justly, for we are receiving what we deserve for our deeds; but this man has done nothing wrong."* After coming to the Lord, we <u>do</u> have that fear of God… like a child has a fear and respect of their loving father (fear that if we don't do what is right in his eyes we will disappoint him and cause him <u>to have</u> to discipline us). We also defend the Lord and our faith. We rebuke those that would come against Him. Most of all, we realize that we are guilty of sin and that we deserved the punishment that He took in our place.

Luke 23:42, the opening verse, is the key to what the Lord desires of us. The criminal (sinner) knew that he was wrong. He also knew that Jesus was a King and that He could have mercy and forgive him; remember him; love him. We also, as believers, know these things to be true.

Luke 23:43 - *And He said to him, "Truly I say to you, today you shall be with Me in Paradise."* Because of the criminal's faith in who Jesus was, even though condemned to die for his crimes, he was saved.

When I read these verses, I always get teary eyed. First, because of the faith of the second criminal. He is going through what has been described as the worst form of execution ever devised by man. Yet, during that suffering, and somehow knowing that Jesus <u>could</u> save his physical life, instead he accepted his circumstances and he asked for Jesus' compassion and to be with Him in eternity. His plea was for his spiritual life not earthly gain! That is the epitome of how we are to be as Christians. We're to seek first God's kingdom (Matthew 6:33) even when facing something as crucial as death.

The second reason I get teary eyed is because <u>Jesus gives</u> that compassion. We don't know what this man did but it was severe enough to warrant him being crucified. Yet Jesus overlooked his sins. Why? Because the criminal first recognized that he was a sinner. Second, he knew that Jesus was His redemption and asked Him for His forgiveness; the very basics of Christianity.

If you ever are witnessing to someone who feels they can't be forgiven, maybe sharing this parallel will show them that even though they are sinners, Jesus is willing to forgive them and save them.

ANXIOUSLY WAITING

Jude 1:21 *Keep yourselves in the love of God, waiting anxiously for the mercy of our Lord Jesus Christ to eternal life.*

We live in a hurry up society. We have fast food; high speed internet; drive through banking (and even on-line banking so you can spend your money quicker). Where will it all end?

The disciples probably asked that same question as they were celebrating Passover with Jesus in the upper room. The past three years must have seemed like a whirlwind to them. But then... not 24 hours later, Jesus was dead. Crucified like a common criminal and hurriedly buried. Now what? It's Shabbat (Sabbath) and it must have seemed like such a long day. Every little noise, every twitching shadow had them on the edge of their seat. "Are they coming for <u>us</u> now!?"

They had seen Jesus' miracles and heard His teachings from His own lips. Yet, they didn't understand that He would rise from the dead. Saturday for them was a day of sadness and confusion. It was a day of fear and memories. What it wasn't for them was a day of anxiously awaiting His resurrection. They didn't yet know, or at least understand, the whole story (John 20:9).

We do know the whole story. So why are we not anxiously awaiting His return? Or, at least, we should be anxiously waiting for His mercy to eternal life as we're told in Jude 1:21. We, as followers and believers, are given the promise of eternal life when we leave this earth. Jude describes what believers should be doing while waiting:

Jude 1:20: *Build up your faith.* How? Read your Bible and pray daily. Go to church! Listen to and watch things that aren't offensive to God. Let your friendships be with fellow believers… you need to go into the world, but don't be a part of it.

Jude 1:20: *Pray in the Holy Spirit.* This is more than just reciting your wish list to God. This is getting deep with God and desiring Him to get deep with you and not letting go until He does. Think of Jacob wrestling with God and not letting go until, in Jacob's case, God blessed him. Genesis 32:21

Jude 1:21: *Keep yourselves in the love of God?* Don't allow your walk with Him to grow cold. Don't allow the flesh to cause you to pull away from what He has planned for you. King Saul for example: He was chosen by God. But then, because of his disobedience to God, lost what God had given him. (1 Samuel 15)

I feel that Genesis 32:22 & 23 can be looked at together: We have an obligation to watch out for others. We need to show mercy and compassion to struggling believers and also to the unsaved. *Snatching them out of the fire*, as Jude says. But we are also told that there are times that we need to put the fear of God in them. We are to be firm and bold with them (still with compassion).

Although the disciples didn't know to anxiously await for the Lord's resurrection let us be anxious for His return to gather us together (1 Thessalonians 4:16 – 17). Let us also be anxious for His merciful gift of eternal life. However, let's not be idle but do those things described by Jude while we are waiting.

RESURRECTION SUNDAY

John 20:17 *Jesus said to her (Mary Magdalene), "Stop clinging to Me, for I have not yet ascended to the Father; but go to My brethren and say to them, 'I ascend to My Father and your Father, and My God and your God.'"*

We have a fairly new granddaughter in our lives. She is as precious as can be and we have fallen in love with her. However, she, in turn, only wants mom. Take her out of sight from mom and let the crying begin. Although not as severe as with outsiders, even when she is with dad she still wants the security and comfort of mom. When mom is within earshot of the crying, she can't bear to hear her baby in distress. She comes and calms her and loves on her.

In John 20:17, above, one of the things that stick out to me is Jesus telling Mary to, *"Stop clinging to Me..."* Physical contact between a man and woman, that weren't husband and wife, in those days was not tolerated. So, what was happening here?

Mary had seen, first hand, how Jesus had confronted the religious people of the day. How he told them that feeding the hungry or healing the afflicted on the Sabbath was more important than following the letter of the law. Perhaps a physical embrace of her Lord at that moment was more important than the scrutiny that she would receive from any that might see her. However, if you read the verse carefully, it never says, or even implies, that she physically embraced Jesus.

I don't believe that her clinging was physical. Joshua 23:8 says; *"...you are to cling to the LORD your God..."* and Psalm 63:8 says; *"My soul clings to You; Your right hand upholds me."* These verses definitely aren't referring to a physical clinging. It's about a spiritual clinging. I believe Mary's soul now felt the salvation power and the love that radiated from the resurrected Jesus. Mary's spirit, her soul, every part of her being was not only clinging to Him, but didn't want to let go. Jesus had to break the bond by telling her that there is one more step in our total restoration through Him. He had to ascend and take His place next to the Father and prepare a home for her and us. (John 14:2 – 3)

Like our little granddaughter clings to her mom, thus we should be clinging to our Lord. We shouldn't allow strangers, or even other familiar faces, to take His place in giving us security and comfort. We need to think (and rightly so) that His love supersedes all others. Mary understood... at least in her spirit. Jesus had died and now had returned to her and she wasn't letting go this time. Only with His reassurance did she then go and tell the others that He was risen.

Even if you're reading this and today isn't Resurrection Sunday, reflect and remember what Jesus did for you on that wonderful, marvelous day. As you do, allow yourself to be drawn closer to Him to the point that you are clinging to Him and don't want to ever let go. If anyone or anything should try and keep you from seeing Him; let the crying begin! Like mom with the grandbaby... Jesus will come and comfort you and love on you!

WHO'S BEARING THE CROSS

Luke 23:26 *When they led Him away, they seized a man, Simon of Cyrene, coming in from the country, and placed on him the cross to carry behind Jesus.*

The crosses used in crucifixions weren't very light. The main vertical center beam alone was probably, at least, 8 to 10 feet long (maybe slightly longer) and probably, at minimum, the width and breadth of a modern 4 by 4. The horizontal cross beam would have been the same width and breadth but probably only 4 to 6 feet in length. It's estimated that an assembled cross could have weighed as much as 300 pounds. There are accounts that the condemned would only carry the horizontal cross beam (only weighing about 100 pounds) to a site where the vertical beams would already be in place. The horizontal beam would then be raised and set atop of the vertical beam with the victim already nailed to it. We're told in 3 of the 4 gospels that Simon from Cyrene was forced to carry Jesus' cross.

In Luke 9:23, Jesus says, *"If anyone wishes to come after Me, he must deny himself, and take up his cross daily and follow Me."* That's not an easy task. The physical cross was a heavy burden to carry. Simon experienced that while following Jesus to Golgotha. Jesus tells us to take up our spiritual cross, (Those things that would cause us to suffer, that would hinder us, that would try and discourage us in our Christian walk.) daily, and follow Him. What is your cross and how heavy is it?

Your cross may be a physical issue with you or someone very close to you. It may be financial problems or a failing business. It could be a broken home or some other type of relationship trouble. Maybe it's a cry for a spiritual healing of a child or spouse. Perhaps it's a personal spiritual matter or a difficult ministry that God has called you to. Whatever it may be, you need to bear it, even though it may be very heavy on you, and continue to follow Jesus. Although we're told that Simon carried His cross, think of the greater weight that Jesus bore. ... The sins of the world for eternity! For a normal person, that would crush them.

Paul tells us in Philippians 4:7 (KJV) *And the peace of God, which passeth all understanding, shall keep your hearts and minds through Christ Jesus.* We're told that that peace comes when we release our anxieties to the Lord through prayer (and supplication – a very deep, earnest, humble prayer) with THANKSGIVING. In short: When we truly seek the Lord about our circumstances and give Him thanks regardless of them, He helps to bear the weight of our cross (the way Simon did for Him) and thus gives us a peace. Don't be misled... the cross may still be there. He just helps us to bear it. No matter what is going on in your life right now, it's important to continue to give the Lord His praise.

In 2 Corinthians 12 Paul is suffering a "Thorn in the flesh", and as a result is given a promise: (Vs 9) *"My grace is sufficient for you, for power is perfected in weakness."* As we go through weaknesses, insults, distresses, tribulations, persecutions and difficulties, for Christ's sake... we can rely on that same promise Paul received. Allow Christ's power to be made perfect in you even (and especially) during those times when that cross is extra heavy and you feel weak.

PASSOVER

Luke 22:15 *And Jesus said to them, "I have earnestly desired to eat this Passover with you before I suffer;"*

The Passover Seder is still celebrated in many Jewish homes. It is a wonderful celebration of our God, His mercies and His greatness. I would urge any Christian to attend a Seder (or even a Seder teaching) that is open to the public. It is usually around Easter, but sometimes can fall as late as a month later. Before you attend, though, take some time to study for yourself. That way, you'll know if the Seder/teaching is accurate. My wife and I have been invited to a Seder that was not a Seder. It turned out to be more of a church gathering for fellowship and a meal. Not that that's a bad thing… but don't advertise it as a Seder.

I'm not going to go through the Seder here. I do encourage you to purchase the Haggadah which is the book that is used to guide the Seder. It gives step by step instructions on conducting the Seder including what foods are to be eaten and when and why. It also gives the scriptures that are read.

In Luke 22:15 (above) it tells us that Jesus earnestly wanted to share the Passover with His disciples. The Passover was important to Jesus:

> ➢ First, because He was Jewish and that is an important holiday in the Jewish religion which celebrates the Lord passing over the

Israelites on the evening that He put the firstborn of all of Egypt to death (Read Exodus 12:1 – 51).

➤ Second, because of the significance of the celebration and how it relates to Jesus and what He did for us and how He became our Passover lamb.

- o The breaking of the Matzah and hiding it (As Jesus was broken and then hidden away in the tomb). (1 Corinthians 11:23, 24 & 26)

- o How when the Matzah is found by the children that the celebration can continue. If they don't find it… the Passover celebration is over. If we, as God's children, find Jesus… then the celebration begins. If we don't, then death doesn't pass us over, but consumes us.

- o The bitter herbs can loosely represent the bitter drink Jesus was offered on the cross.

- o The third cup… known as the 'Cup of Redemption', was the cup that Jesus said: *"This cup is the new covenant in My blood; do this, as often as you drink it, in remembrance of Me."* (1 Corinthians 11:25) He was telling His disciples that the shedding of His blood was going to be their (and our) redemption.

  - • Side Note: When Jesus said; *"This is the covenant in My blood…"*, His disciples would have recognized that those were the same words used when a young man, of that time, would propose marriage to a young girl. One interpretation is that He was asking them to be His bride.

That is just some of what you can learn from attending a Messianic Seder or Seder teaching. It shows that Jesus was also very much a part of the old testament and proof that He is the Messiah.

IN YOUR FACE EVANGELISM?

Matthew 10:16 (KJV) *Behold, I send you forth as sheep in the midst of wolves: be ye therefore wise as serpents, and harmless as doves.*

I have attended a few Passover Seders in the past. Most were done by a Messianic Jewish pastor. One was by a good friend at his home... he did a very good job at explaining the Passover and using scripture as he performed the Seder.

There was one, however, that my wife and I were invited to that was very off base. It was at a Christian church with no Jewish background and wound up being more about the meal then what Passover represents. The problem we had (thinking that this Passover ceremony would equal our past experiences)... we invited a Jewish friend hoping to do some evangelizing. Instead, it was a disaster. On top of the Passover ceremony being a bust, one of the members of the church got in our Jewish friends face and was practically yelling at him and condemning him for not seeing that Jesus was the Messiah. It seemed that all of the prep work that my wife and I had done prior to that was erased by this very confused Christian lady.

There is an old saying: One can catch more flies with honey than you can with vinegar. What that means is if you want to influence someone to see or do what you would like them to, it is better to be nice rather than 'in their face'.

This also holds true in evangelizing. Although we know that Jesus is the only way, the world won't accept that unless it is presented to them in a positive manner. As evangelists, we need to share the good news with the unsaved and not the condemnations of their false beliefs. The Lord may have you instruct them in those things later... but, even then, they should be conveyed in a loving way.

I think of how Jesus ministered: Yes, He was straight and to the point with the Pharisees, the religious leaders of the time, because He had to be. But when it came to the layman; there are many examples of His patience and love in dealing with them. One example I can think of is in John 4. Jesus meets a Samaritan woman at a well and engages her in conversation by asking that she fetch him a drink. As the conversation proceeds, we find that she has had 5 husbands and is now living with a man out of wedlock. Note that Jesus doesn't condemn her for this! Instead He tells her that He is the living water and the Messiah. As a result, the woman went to the city and called others to come and see this Jesus. In John 4:39 – 41, we find that many of the Samaritans then believed. Once they became believers, then it would fall on them to study Jesus' ways and to walk the walk He set before them.

The Samaritans believed that they knew the true worship of God as practiced by Abraham and that the other Israelites of the time were practicing altered worship due to a tainting during their exile to Babylon. This was a major conflict of the time and Jesus could have easily got in the woman's face, the way that the woman at the failed Seder did to our friend. Instead He used wisdom and gentleness with her. Look at the results. He gave us a wonderful example of how to tell our unsaved friends about the gospel. As we do, we need to be wise and gentle. They may not have wings and buzz but I bet they will be more attracted to sweetness over vinegar.

CHRISTMAS TIDBITS

Christmas is a favorite holiday of many. I admit that it is one of my favorite holidays. Not because of the gifts; far from that reason! But because of the closeness and love that is felt at that time of year. People seem to put away their differences for a while, and come together to celebrate. In too many cases, that celebration is of a worldly nature. But, one of the other reasons that it is one of my favorites is because people, that aren't walking with Christ, are open to hearing the gospel message as long as the Christmas story is attached to it. I love Cloverton's version of "Christmas Hallelujah". The first 4 verses tell of Jesus' birth. The last verse gives the reason for His being born; so that He could one day die for our sins and give us salvation and redemption.

The next 10 tidbits reference Christmas. I've dated them so that, if you desire, you can read the tidbit for that particular day. However, those dates are just a suggestion. Feel free to read them as you would like.

BTW: Merry Christmas!

DECEMBER 20TH - A GOOD STEWARD

Mark 12:31 *"The second is this, 'YOU SHALL LOVE YOUR NEIGHBOR AS YOURSELF.' There is no other commandment greater than these."*

I love Charles Dickens, "A Christmas Carol". It is such a wonderful story of redemption and the journey that Scrooge had to take to find it. He had to see himself as others saw him… miserly, crotchety and just out and out mean. He had made money his god and he served it well. Instead, Marley's ghost tells Scrooge who he should have been serving in this excerpt from Charles Dickens, "A Christmas Carol":

But you were always a good man of business, Jacob,' faltered Scrooge, who now began to apply this to himself. 'Business!' cried the Ghost, wringing its hands again. 'Mankind was my business. The common welfare was my business; charity, mercy, forbearance, and benevolence, were, all, my business. The dealings of my trade were but a drop of water in the comprehensive ocean of my business!'

As Christians, we are called to be "good stewards" of what God has given us. A Biblical definition of a good steward: to manage God's resources, especially those that He has put in our immediate care, in a way that will please Him. Are you a good steward of what God has given you? Do you faithfully tithe and even give extra as an offering? That's good if you do, but there is more to being a good steward.

Let's look at one of the biggest misconceptions of being a good steward. That is that you have to be miserly... like Scrooge. As Jesus says in Matthew 6:19 – 20, those tangible things that we hold on too tightly to will, one day, be destroyed. There are greater treasures in heaven.

It's important to not put yourself in, what I call, the church box. You tithe and only give to those things that the church supports. What about those around us? Do you ask your neighbors what they are in need of? And when they tell you, do you offer to help? Or, is that someone else's business!? Mankind should be our business, as Marley's ghost exclaimed to Scrooge. The opening scripture also supports this: You wouldn't be stingy with yourself, so why be stingy with those around you?

Unfortunately, I even hear of churches that are like that. They will give to missionaries and other ministries (within their box), but neglect to take care of their own (Reference Acts 6:1 as an example). This includes: members of their congregation; church staff (raises and benefits); other local needs not associated with the church. The excuse is not that they don't have the resources... instead it is that they are being good stewards (by not spending money). In reality, their stewardship is in question.

In short, being a good steward can mean being stingy with stuff, when that is what is warranted. But, it more so means to use what you have wisely even if that means giving extra to those that God has put in your path so that you can be a blessing to them. To make them a part of your business. This applies to both corporate and to individual management of what you have. It not only blesses in the natural, but is a great spiritual encouragement and, maybe even, a witness that can bring salvation and redemption. If you're going to act like Scrooge, than do so as he was on Christmas morning following his redemption. Be a good steward; Be about the business of mankind.

DECEMBER 21ST - DIVINE APPOINTMENT

Acts 8:29 *Then the Spirit said to Philip, "Go up and join this chariot."*

I have a good friend that used to be on a very popular local Christian television program. Christmas was approaching and he was given an assignment to go to a popular area of town and interview people on the street, asking; "What does Christmas mean to you?" My friend was worried about not getting enough Christian responses. He asked me if I would be able to stop by during the couple of hours that he was set up and be interviewed. I happily agreed to do it.

Where he was taping is known as Market Square in Pittsburgh, PA. It is almost impossible to not find someone in that area, especially when there is a second person holding a big professional television camera. Notice, I said ALMOST impossible. I rode around Market Square a few times without seeing a trace of my friend. I finally parked my car and started walking.

Not too many steps into my venture, I was approached by a young man asking me for some change for bus fare. What the young man didn't know was that I had been in this area many times doing homeless and evangelistic outreaches. I was well aware that was the common way beggars used to get money from "soft hearted" people. Then it would be spent to buy alcohol, cigarettes or drugs. I told him that I was wise to his ploy and then asked him, "What do you really want the money for?"

"If I tell you, will you give it to me?" he asked. I reiterated my question. "For a bottle of wine", he answered. When I told him that I wouldn't give it to him, he tried to turn it around on me as if I had agreed to give the money to him if he was honest. I told him that he knows that was not what I said.

I then began witnessing to him and then offered to buy him some food. We went together into a nearby bagel shop and he got a sandwich and a drink. When we exited I told him to wait there... there was something I wanted to give him. I went to my car and got a tract and a pocket Bible. As I went back toward him, he was with several other men. He immediately left them and came to meet me. "Don't go over there. They will all try and hit you up for money." I handed him the Bible and tract. "My grandmother has been trying to get me saved for years," he said. "I hear what you're saying and I really do appreciate you buying me food and taking the time to talk to me. But, I'm not there yet. I'll read these and who knows." He let me pray for him and then we parted company.

As he walked away, I looked over at a street corner that I had driven by a few times and there stood my friend and his camera man. I went up to him and asked how long he had been there. At least an hour he said.

As the Holy Spirit spoke to Philip in Acts 8, and told him to go to the eunuch and then the eunuch was saved, I feel that this encounter was also a divine appointment. I was blinded to my friend so that I could meet this other young man. I really do expect to see him in heaven one day.

Be sensitive to the Holy Spirit's leading. Don't judge the person He leads you to. He sees their heart! Had I blown off the young man, judging him for wanting money for booze... it would've been my loss.

DECEMBER 22ND - WHERE TO DRAW THE LINE

Hebrews 4:12 *For the word of God is living and active and sharper than any two-edged sword, and piercing as far as the division of soul and spirit, of both joints and marrow, and able to judge the thoughts and intentions of the heart.*

Sadly, it is around the holidays that our church receives telephone calls from people asking for money. The need for the money varies from wanting to buy presents for their children, to paying the rent and/or utilities, to buying food. It's not my place to judge whether there is sincerity in the need or not... that's between those asking and God. We do want to be sensitive to someone who does have a need, but since we are not sure, we have a rule: The person asking needs to come to our church so that we can get to know them. (This helps us to know if they really do have a need and if so, we have a fund set up for that purpose.)

I try to explain to them that if we would give to everyone that calls, we wouldn't even be able to help those in our body that have similar needs. We would quickly run out of funds. With that said, we also try to be sensitive to the Holy Spirit. We have given when we felt prompted by Him. We also try and guide them to practical help; IE: food banks; homeless shelters; utility help lines; etc.

When we do turn people down, we've gotten a wide range of responses. I've had people very politely say thank you. I've also had people, literally, cuss me out and ask me how I could call myself a Christian.

We're not to judge hearts. Yes, we can judge sin and actions… but when it comes to motives; that's Gods job. According to Hebrews 4:12 (above), He uses His word in doing so. How? When we invite those wanting a handout from our church to come to church, we are inviting them to get to know God's word. They will hear that word preached and will be instructed to study it for themselves. They will see God's perspective of what they are doing through the word. In the process, if their intentions aren't pure, they will hopefully turn to Jesus and from their ways and repent (2 Chronicles 2:14). If their motives are pure and honest, then I know that God will use our church to bless them. I know that the hearts of the bulk of our congregation are hearts that desire to give.

It is difficult to turn away someone who may seem very sincere. Again, that is where we need to be in touch with the Spirits leading. If we just give and are taken advantage of, even personally and not just the church, then we are doing as much of an injustice to that person as if we know that someone is truly in need and we do nothing. At the least, we are endorsing that person's laziness and lying. Even worse, we may be supporting that person's habit (drugs; alcohol; gambling; etc.).

Be wise this Christmas when you may be approached by a stranger with their hand out. Jesus told His disciples: (Matthew 10:16) *Behold, I send you out as sheep in the midst of wolves; so be shrewd as serpents and innocent as doves.* Be sensitive to the Spirit's leading or His warning.

DECEMBER 23RD - CHRISTMAS CAROLS

Matthew 2:11b *and they (the Magi) fell to the ground and worshiped Him.*

Even in my BC days (That's what I call the period in my life before I was saved... BC = Before Christ) I loved Christmas music. I would begin listening to it on October 1st. I had several Christmas 8 tracks that would find their way into the car and get played over and over. OK, I know that I'm dating myself by admitting to having 8 tracks. That gives you an idea as to how long ago that was. I have never stopped loving Christmas music.

There are a couple of radio stations in my area that begin playing Christmas music, non-stop, around Thanksgiving and they don't stop playing it until midnight, December 26th. I keep those stations programmed on my car radio during that time. It is such a letdown when I get in my car the day after Christmas, hit the presets for those stations and hear regular secular music on them. I haven't yet stopped wanting to celebrate the Lord's birth.

I know that there are different aspects of Christmas music. Some of the songs tell of Santa Claus; his elves or his reindeer; of secular Christmas celebrations; and some are just about winter and snow. I have to admit, I do listen to them all. When a Christmas song comes on, though, that tells of our Lord's birth and glorifies God, then it becomes personal. It's those songs that I listen to the words and, many times, sing along praising our God.

The Christmas songs that do tell of Christ <u>are</u> hymns. Many were written with the intent to worship the Lord and not just be sung as fun seasonal songs. With that thought, there are people who wouldn't think of listening to a Christian radio station playing Christian music. However, during this time of year, they are hearing hymns being sung to our God almost everywhere that they go. Without thinking about it, they may even start singing along.

We as Christians need to go a step further. We need to think about the words and worship Him. In Matthew 2:11, the Magi, when they saw Him, fell to the ground and worshiped Him. Let the music you hear during the Christmas season draw you into a deeper worship.

We think of Jesus' sacrifice on the cross, but remember that it was also a sacrifice for God to humble Himself to the point of becoming flesh (John 1:14). In reality, this was as necessary for our way to salvation as was Jesus' death on the cross. So when you hear those Christmas hymns, sing with joy and worship in your heart, giving God the glory that He is due. Worshipping Him for His humble beginnings and giving up His place in heaven just for us.

DECEMBER 24TH - A HUMBLE BIRTH

Luke 2:7 *And she gave birth to her firstborn son; and she wrapped Him in cloths, and laid Him in a manger, because there was no room for them in the inn.*

The words of Luke tell us that our Lord was born in the humblest of conditions. So what was it like?

Mary and Joseph had to travel to Bethlehem, where Joseph was from, because of a census. Joseph would have probably still had family there and in that culture it would have been customary for those relatives to open their house to family members. We're told that Mary was betrothed to Joseph. In short, they were married (thus the reason the scripture says that Joseph was willing to secretly DIVORCE Mary). However, the marriage wouldn't be consummated until about a year following the engagement at a traditional wedding ceremony. Joseph's relatives could have done the math as to how pregnant Mary was and either suspected that Joseph and Mary had sex prior to the wedding or that Mary had been unfaithful to him. Can it be because of that, that Mary and Joseph may have been shunned by Joseph's family and not welcomed into their house?

As a result, we read that Mary gave birth and Jesus was laid in a manger because there was no room in the inn (Luke 2:7). This implies that Jesus was born in a stable (although the word stable isn't used in the scriptures, that is where you will find most mangers = a feeding or watering trough for animals). What was the stable? Chances are it wasn't the cute little wooden structure that you find with most modern day nativity sets. Wood is a scarce commodity in Israel; even today. To use it to build a structure to house animals wouldn't have been practical. Instead caves would be used as stables. It wouldn't have been well lit and would have probably smelled pretty bad.

As for the manger… On my first visit to Israel, we were able to see a manager from Jesus' time in ancient Capernaum. As stated above, since wood is scarce in Israel, the manger we saw was carved out of stone. Our teacher told us that the stone manger was common back in Jesus' time. Chances are, that is what the shepherds saw baby Jesus lying in when they paid their visit that night. (Side note: Shepherds back in Jesus' time were much like the present day Bedouin shepherds found in Israel. Many of them are young girls. Just something to think about.)

One true depiction that you will find in a modern nativity set… there may have been animals in the stable. Depending on the size of the cave, there could have been sheep; donkeys; camels; cows; and/or even fowl (although not mentioned in scripture, archaeological digs have found chicken bones in Israel dating as far back as King Solomon).

Think about it: In a dimly lit cave (at best) with animal noises, messes and smells and laid in a stone trough (BTW: there may or may not have been straw in the manger. If so, it may not have been very clean straw); that's how our Lord started His journey to set us free. The ultimate humility shown out of a love that boggles my mind. That's our God!

My final thought is of Mary. How, between contractions, she must have thought of the angelic visit that she received 9 months earlier. The message that the child that she was delivering this night was to be Emmanuel. Most would think that God would provide a better place for His Son to be born. But, the circumstances don't cause Mary's faith to waiver. How humble she was in giving birth to our humble savior.

DECEMBER 25TH - A BIRTHDAY CELEBRATION

Matthew 1:25b *she gave birth to a Son; and he called His name Jesus.*

Christmas is, in fact, a man made holiday and not one found in the scriptures. So, is it wrong for Christians to celebrate Christmas? This is a debate that has been going on for centuries. Here's my take on it: Christmas is supposed to be a celebration of Christ's birth. I don't feel that the 25th of December is His true birthday. However, why shouldn't we celebrate His birth? Without His birth, nothing else in the gospels would have happened and we would be lost forever.

We celebrate other people's birthdays and even celebrity's birthdays? President's Day, for example, was originally designated to celebrate George Washington's birthday. Abraham Lincoln's birthday was celebrated a week earlier, prior to the Uniform Monday Holiday Act when both of those birthdays were combined. Now all presidents are honored on that day. I'm not saying whether we should or shouldn't honor them, but, who are they compared to Jesus!?

As for the date not being correct; I know a couple that couldn't have children. Because of the red tape in the U. S., when it comes to adopting, they chose to adopt from China... twice. There was no record of either child's actual birth date, but, the doctors in the U. S. were able to determine the approximate date of birth. The couple then picked a date close to the children's estimated birthdates. They now celebrate the birth of those children (my two wonderful and beautiful nieces) every year on those dates.

I know that there are those that have a problem with the modern customs and traditions. Okay… don't participate in them. You can still pay homage to Jesus' birth by sharing the true story of that event to others without doing anything that you might feel uncomfortable doing. People are very receptive at this time of the year to listen to the whole gospel message when it's tied in with the Christmas story. This is a wonderful time of year for evangelism. …*do the work of an evangelist, fulfill your ministry.* (2 Timothy 4:5b)

One tradition that we started on our gathering at Christmas, is to share the gospel concerning the truth of Christ's birth (I will usually share one of my tidbits about Christmas). We do have family that aren't saved. Sharing the true picture of that night in Bethlehem is a way to get them to think of what they may be missing by only celebrating the traditional aspects of the day. We are giving meaning to what really happened that night and what Jesus' ultimate purpose was by coming to Earth as a man.

In the opening scripture… *"…she gave birth to a Son"…* What wonderful words to read! What a glorious day it was! Let's celebrate it and in the process, share its true meaning to OPEN HEARTS (in hope that the Holy Spirit will soon dwell there)!

DECEMBER 26ᵀᴴ - WISE MEN SEEK HIM

Matthew 2:11a *After coming into the house they (Magi) saw the Child with Mary His mother;*

Interesting facts about the Magi:

1) The Greek word for Magi is Magos. This was a name given to a wide variety of people by various Middle Eastern tribes. The name would have been given to wise men; astronomers; soothsayers; teachers; priests; interpreters of dreams; sorcerers and others.

2) Since we're told that they were from the east (Matthew 2:1), they could have been from India or China. Or maybe even closer... from what is present day Iran or Iraq.

3) They were wealthy... we know this by the gifts that they presented. (Matthew 2:11b)

4) They were all probably from the same country. (In Matthew 2:12 it says that the Magi left for their own COUNTRY (singular) by another way.)

Some other facts to contemplate:

The Magi were NOT at the manger;
Let's start with the opening scripture; Matthew 2:1 – It says; *"After coming into the HOUSE they saw the child..."* It doesn't say; after coming into the stable or cave.

In Matthew 2:2, the Magi inquire, *"Where is He who <u>HAS BEEN BORN</u>..."* These words tell us that Jesus was already born when they were still in Jerusalem making their inquiries. Joseph would have gone out the first thing the next morning, following Jesus' birth, to find lodging for Mary, Jesus and himself. They would not have stayed in the stable any longer than necessary.

The next piece of evidence is a little more complex;
When Herod met with the Magi, in Matthew 2:7, it says, *"...he determined from them the exact time the star appeared."* When the Magi didn't return to Herod, we then see his tyranny. Matthew 2:16 *Then when Herod saw that he had been tricked by the magi, he became very enraged, and sent and slew all the male children who were in Bethlehem and all its vicinity, <u>from two years old and under,</u> ACCORDING TO THE TIME WHICH HE HAD DETERMINED FROM THE MAGI.* Herod didn't wait 2 years for the Magi to return and yet he put to death children up to the age of two as determined by what the Magi had told him. Jesus may very well have been one to two years old when the Magi visited him.

Another tidbit concerns the star:
The Magi were NOT following the star at first. They were Magi FROM THE EAST and they saw the star IN THE EAST. (Matthew 2:1 & 2) Had they followed the star from the beginning, they would have been travelling in the wrong direction. It wasn't until after they met with Herod in Jerusalem that we are told that the star <u>led</u> them to where Jesus was. (Matthew 2:9 & 10)

Traditions are fun and this time of year is steeped in them. Am I telling you to put away the Magi from your traditional nativity set? Not at all: I don't think it's important to know when exactly the Magi visited Jesus.

I do feel that it is important to know that they were foreigners and yet sought Him. It was a great sacrifice to travel far in those days but they wanted to find the newborn King. Wise people still seek Him today. I hope that you are a wise person!

DECEMBER 27ᵀᴴ - BIRTHDAY GIFTS FOR A KING

Matthew 2:11b *Then, opening their treasures, they presented to Him gifts of gold, frankincense, and myrrh.*

Over the last few years, Kathy and I have been trying to cut back on our spending for gifts at Christmas. It's not because we're poor or miserly. It's because we feel that Christmas has gotten away from its true meaning. Now, I'm not opposed to giving those that I love something as a token of my love. I guess Christmas is as good of a time as any to do that. But is it what Christmas is really about? My answer is; <u>No</u>!

The tradition of giving gifts originated from the Magi's generosity. However, I feel we have forgotten some facts:

➢ One thing that is forgotten is that the Magi's gifts were <u>given to Jesus</u>… not each other.

➢ Another thing that is forgotten; when you celebrate a birthday, who gets the gifts? The answer: The person whose birthday that you're celebrating. (Note: our 5 year old granddaughter made that same observation that Jesus should be getting the gifts.)

How much do we give to Jesus on the day that we celebrate His birthday? Do we go to church for an hour or two? Do we say grace before the

Christmas dinner? Do we listen to spiritual Christmas songs? All good…
but are they truly the best of gifts for our King?

The Bible tells us that He owns the cattle on a thousand hills (Psalm 50:10)
and that He created all things (Revelation 4:11)(which, if He created it, it
must belong to Him). What Birthday gift do you give to someone who,
literally, has everything? Give Him what He desires the most… YOUR
LOVE! (Deuteronomy 6:5)

How do you wrap such a gift? By how you show it:

- Obedience to Him and His word (1 John 5:3)
- Fellowship with Him (Ephesians 6:18 & 1 Thessalonians 5:17)
- Worship of Him (Psalm 150:6)
- Loving others (John 15:12)
- Giving to others that are in need (1 John 3:17 – 18)
- Sharing His story so as to draw others closer to Him (2 Timothy 4:5)

What about the Magi's gifts? Weren't they worldly? No… they gave Jesus
special prophetic gifts. Matthew 2:11 says that they gave Him gold (A
gift for a King; thus acknowledging His royalty); Frankincense (incense
which was symbolic of Deity); and Myrrh (An embalming oil – a symbol
that this new born king has come to offer His life for us). They probably
didn't even know just how special their gifts were to Him.

I know Christmas is over but it's okay to start giving Him next year's
gifts now… all of your love. That way, next December 25th, you can say,
"Happy Birthday Jesus!" and know that you've blessed Him with the best
gift that you can give Him… YOU!

DECEMBER 28TH - AFTER IT'S OVER

Luke 2:30 *For my eyes have seen Your salvation*

I always feel a little sad on the days immediately following Christmas. There's no more Christmas music being played on the radio or at the stores. People are beginning to remove the decorations from their houses. All of the hype and expectations, such as having family and friends over for the holiday, are over. True, New Year's Eve is on its way... but it's not the same.

Yet, if we were living at the time of Jesus' birth and we knew Mary and Joseph, it would be a joyous time. There is a new baby boy to love and care for. And for Mary and Joseph, who were both told by an angel who that baby boy would be, it would be even more joyful.

According to Levitical law, after the birth of a son, the mother would be deemed unclean for 7 days and then there would be a 33 day purification period following that (If you do the math, that equals 40 days total). The boy would have been given his name and circumcised on the eight day after being born. Mary and Joseph, after the 40 days, took Jesus to the temple to make their sacrifices in obedience to the law.

It is then that we read, in Luke 2:25 - 29, about a man named Simeon...

- A man who God had told that he would not see death until he saw the Lord's Christ.
- He went to the temple that day guided by the Holy Spirit.
- He recognized Jesus as God's Salvation for all people. (Luke 2:30 – 31)
- He now had a peace about dying knowing that he has seen the Lord's Christ.

…And a woman named Anna.

- A prophetess that had lost her husband after only 7 years of marriage and remained a widow.
- She was 84 years old and lived in the temple.
- She served with fasting and prayers.
- When she came upon Joseph, Mary, Simeon and Jesus, she began giving thanks to God and spoke of Jesus to those looking for the redemption of Jerusalem.

Although we may have a letdown once Christmas is over, Simeon and Anna found joy following the birth of Jesus. They knew that the real work of God was just beginning and that our Salvation and redemption was at hand.

We know things that Simeon and Anna didn't know though: We know how Jesus accomplished that salvation for us… through the cross. We know that He has given us instructions and wisdom through His Word… the Bible.

We need to continue to rejoice in the days following Christmas just as Simeon and Anna did. For our true joy is in the fact that Christ is our salvation and redemption.

Maybe not physically, as with Simeon; but my spiritual eyes have seen God's salvation.

DECEMBER 29TH - NO GIFT RECEIPT

Ephesians 2:8 *For by grace you have been saved through faith; and that not of yourselves, it is the gift of God;*

At Christmas, it is customary to give and receive gifts with people that you know and care about. Sometimes, though, there are reasons to return a gift. After Christmas, stores set up special counters for returns. I remember, some years back, going into a popular department store and seeing several temporary return counters set up and long lines at each one. Obviously there were a lot of people who were dissatisfied with Christmas gifts that they had received. There are many reasons for those returns:

1) Doesn't fit.
2) Already have one.
3) Doesn't work.
4) Don't really like it.
5) It's okay, but there is something else I really want that I can exchange this for.
6) Don't need it.

Nowadays stores make it easier to return stuff. They will print out gift receipts at the time of the purchase (which the gift giver puts in the package with the gift). The special return counters are diminishing also because a lot of stores are accepting returns at any of the regular checkout registers.

Our God is also a giver of gifts. He only gives good gifts that we should never want to return: Luke 11:13 *If you then, being evil, know how to give good gifts to your children, how much more will your heavenly Father give the Holy Spirit to those who ask Him?*

In the opening scripture above, He gives His grace as a gift so that we can have salvation. But, as with the natural gifts that we give and get because of someone's relationship with us, our part to receive that gift of grace is to have a relationship with and faith in Jesus. To acknowledge who He is, what He did for us (so that we might be saved) and to totally trust Him as Lord in our lives.

If you received His gift of grace then you've received Him. There is no good reason to return that gift: He fits <u>ALL</u> (Acts 10:36)

1) Already have one?! (1 Chronicles 16:25 – 26)
2) Doesn't work? (Philippians 1:6)
3) Don't really like it? (Deuteronomy 6:5)
4) Something else you really want? (Exodus 20:2a & 3)
5) Don't need it? (John 14:6)

There is no gift receipt for God's gift to you. If you've received God's gift of grace, you need to now give Him a gift back. First and foremost, He wants your love! What a wonderful gift that is to give to our God! But He also wants to spread His gift around and He wants you to help Him to do that by telling others how they can receive it (Share His Word with all - 2 Timothy 4:5).

If you haven't already, receive His gift today! I promise that it will be a gift you won't want to return.

Printed in the United States
By Bookmasters